The Lost Summer

The Lost Summer

A personal memoir of
F. Scott Fitzgerald

Tony Buttitta

Foreword by Bryan Forbes

St. Martin's Press
New York

This book is for

MONICA

who inspired it

MALCOLM COWLEY

who discovered it

BRYAN FORBES

who revived it

and

MELINA

for her faith

Acknowledgment is made to the following for permission to quote material:
MICROCARD EDITIONS BOOKS: *Scott: One More Emotion* by Anthony Buttitta.
Copyright © 1972 by National Cash Register Company. THE VIKING PRESS, INC.: From
"Watching the Needleboats at San Sabba" from *The Portable James Joyce.* Copyright
1927 by James Joyce. All rights reserved. Reprinted by permission of The Viking
Press, Inc.

   Part of this material originally appeared in a different form, 1935 to 1962, in *The
Saturday Review of Literature, The New York Times, The Raleigh News and
Observer, The Charlotte News, The Asheville News, The Durban Herald-Sun, The
San Francisco Chronicle,* and the United Press (now UPI). The first two chapters of
the memoir have been published in the *Fitzgerald/Hemingway Annual,* 1972.

Library of Congress Cataloging-in-Publication Data

Buttitta, Tony.
   The lost summer.

   1. Fitzgerald, F. Scott (Francis Scott),
1896–1940—Biography.   2. Buttitta, Tony—Friends
and associates.   3. Authors, American—20th
century—Biography.   I. Title.
PS3511.19Z5724   1987   813'.52   [B]   87-13975
ISBN 0-312-01061-3 (pbk.)

Originally published under the title *After the Good Gay Times*

First published in Great Britain by Robson Books Ltd.

First U.S. Edition

10 9 8 7 6 5 4 3 2 1

To chance upon a little-known book and to be able to pluck it from obscurity, is to me akin to the joy an archaeologist must feel when he unlocks the secrets of a tomb. From early childhood when I cycled once a day to forage for books in West Ham Public Library, or else haunted a Dickensian second-hand bookshop for halfpenny bargains, the printed word has always obsessed me. Perhaps because I have been fortunate enough to make a living as a writer, the biographies, autobiographies and journals of other writers hold a particular fascination: possibly it stems from a need to be assured that we all share the same common nightmares— that wrestling with the blank sheet of paper when the sap of creation does not flow; the conviction that at any given moment it will dry up for ever. Writing is one of the loneliest of the arts; unlike the actor we have no immediate audience and must wait many long months, even years on occasion, for the splatter of applause to reach our ears, if indeed we are not damned by total neglect.

So, many years ago, when I was filming in Hollywood, I chanced upon a slim volume by an author hitherto unknown to me. The title was *After the Good Gay Times* (alas, today, open to false interpretation). The jacket blurb informed me it was written by a one-time bookseller named Tony Buttitta and that it was concerned with a little-known episode in the tragic life of F. Scott Fitzgerald. As with so many other struggling writers of my generation, to me Fitzgerald epitomised the glory and the injustice of a writer's lot, for the young are always attracted to heroic failures. I read Tony Buttitta's memoir at a single sitting and immediately attempted to secure the film rights, for the story he told with such sympathy and candour suggested a screenplay to me.

For reasons that time has obscured, nothing came of my attempts to obtain the rights. It could be that I found no takers amongst the illiterates who then controlled the major studios, for few of them betrayed any evidence that they were capable of comprehending anything in print other than a contract criminally weighted in their favour.

Although I kept a copy of the book on my shelves and from time to time took it down to reread, another decade passed before I finally made contact with the author. It so happened that, out of the blue, he wrote me a generous fan letter concerning a novel I had written, and when replying I enquired as to the fate of his own book. He wrote back that the only American edition had long been out of print. In the interim, of course, a veritable Scott Fitzgerald cottage industry had sprung up. At his death, Fitzgerald was a spent force, virtually written off by publishers and public alike. The dapper, ambitious young man with the soft, almost feminine, features had disintegrated into the middle-aged alcoholic. The early vision of paradise had never been regained and he died struggling to record a world that had rejected him, for his last efforts were directed at charting a Hollywood indifferent to his unique talents. Despite passages of great beauty and perception, the unfinished *The Last Tycoon* is the work of an outsider, the perennial romantic staring through the window at a party he was not invited to.

Now his reputation rests securely on *The Great Gatsby*, and a dozen of the best short stories in the language. Yet there is a blanket of sadness that covers his posthumous fame as surely as the alcoholic fog that obscured so much of his life. Like a swarm of hungry bees the biographers have descended on his meagre store of nectar and plundered it. His life has been laid bare as few writers' before: we now know every intimate and frequently sordid detail of his rise and fall—he lies before us like a ruined city where any scavenger may wander. Every year new volumes appear, many merely rehashing old myths, adding little to our understanding of the writer but concentrating on the ashes of the man. Recently he received the final accolade of our impoverished age, the television mini-series. Of such is the Kingdom of Heaven.

He first wrote from the desperation of love, for he wished to lay a tribute at the feet of the girl of his dreams: lacking money and position, it was the only gift he had to offer in order to win her hand, and from the very beginning he committed himself to the production of masterpieces. In the event he produced, in Edmund Wilson's words, "one of the most illiterate books of any merit ever published," and married the girl. Together, they first enraptured and then destroyed each other, becoming in the process the chief exponents of what was called The Jazz Age. Life, for a time, was an almost continuous party. They were the principal guests, playing their roles with a theatrical innocence, cherishing the promises that life held out in seemingly inexhaustible quantities. They even made preparations for when the party would end: Fitzgerald set a deadline of age thirty for his own suicide, periodically advancing the date to fifty—a year he failed to reach.

To me the beauty of Tony Buttitta's memoir, which I am privileged to introduce to a wider audience under a less ambiguous title, is that he illuminates some of the dark corners of Fitzgerald's tortured life—his remembrance of things past reads like a novel that his principal character might well have written. It is a book about love and loyalty wrapped around a man who was ultimately denied both; a man who constantly sought the bluebird of happiness, and brought about his self-destruction in the quest.

It is always dangerous to make claims in advance, but I would be less than honest if I did not admit that my deep affection and admiration for Mr. Buttita's compelling book leads me to believe it is worthy of revival. It is a modest work, written by a true writer, without affectation and pretensions, and to my mind it answers many of the questions that Fitzgerald's more vaunted biographers left unsolved. In the first place it has not been cobbled together, second-hand, from press-cuttings but forged from a personal relationship. Therein lies its uniqueness.

Mr. Buttitta describes the sad happenings of that lost summer in Asheville with the skill of a born storyteller, and I find it curious that this watershed episode in Fitzgerald's life is barely touched upon in the major biographies, and virtually ignored in most of the other accounts. Fitzgerald took the young bookseller completely into his confidence, baring his soul to a listener who fortunately also had the ability to record their relationship with compassion and a total lack of censure. During those dog days in Asheville, Fitzgerald embarked with an owl and a pussycat on his own turbulent sea. The two women who form the core of this story—one a whore, the other an impressionable, neurotic young girl—gave him a degree of human love, and the author, as Fitzgerald's Boswell, gave him friendship. So for a few brief months these widely diverse lives touched, and then passed on.

To my mind this little-known book reveals more of Fitzgerald than many of the weighty tomes that regularly arrive on our shelves and merely regurgitate familiar material. What Mr. Buttitta encapsulates better than most are the authentic reasons behind the triumph and the tragedy of Fitzgerald's life. The truth was that although he tried hard to die, he tried harder still to succeed. The sad irony is that it was only after death that his true worth was discovered. It is an all too-familiar epitaph for the artist in our midst whom we so shamefully neglect. I often remind myself, as I read the auction reports of yet another record being established, that Van Gogh never sold a single painting in his own lifetime.

It is my hope that Mr. Buttitta, now aged seventy-nine, will yet enjoy a just measure of reflected glory.

Bryan Forbes, 1987

Preface

The basic source material for this memoir is notes I jotted down at the time on the fly-leaves of about sixty books, many of which are still in my library. They comprise a kind of log, but serve the same purpose as a diary. Mostly in Fitzgerald's words, the notes are a record of visits, events, incidents, encounters, phone calls that took place between Fitzgerald, myself, and a few others. These notes have been supplemented by articles and reviews I wrote then and later, by letters, and by the *Contempo* file (1931–1933), which Fitzgerald often looked at when he dropped by the Intimate Bookshop in the George Vanderbilt Hotel.

In spite of the years that have passed, I had no difficulty reproducing his monologues from notes I had scribbled in the books. As a reporter I rarely had taken more than a few lead words; they enabled me to quote dialogue and conversations verbatim in stories and interviews. That Asheville summer had remained in my visual and verbal memory as a key period of my life in the thirties. On reading the notes I drifted back and became completely immersed in the events. Fitzgerald's vital personality, his bold and spirited voice, his words and sweeping gestures, along with the memories, thoughts, and emotions they evoked—all this came back as if I were watching an old movie; as if he had reappeared and was in my presence. It was then that I realized what Proust meant when he said, "In reminiscence my experiences do not fade, they grow more vivid, more beautiful or more ugly, but above all, more significant."

Among the sixty volumes in which I jotted the notes are *Living Authors, The American Caravan, The Story of San Michele, Nijinsky, New Russia's Primer, Ten Days That Shook the World,* Tridon's *Psychoanalysis,* Cheiro's *Language of the Hand,* Isadora Duncan's *My Life,* Henderson's *Bernard Shaw: Playboy and Prophet,* Van de Velde's *Ideal Marriage,* Forsythe's *Redder than the Rose,* and books by Louis Adamic, Sherwood Anderson, Peter Arno, John Peale Bishop, Thomas Boyd, Fielding Burke, James Branch Cabell, Erskine Caldwell, E. E. Cummings, John Dos Passos, Theodore Dreiser, William Faulkner, F. Scott Fitzgerald, Ben Hecht, Joseph Hergesheimer, Langston Hughes, James Joyce, Rockwell Kent, Ring Lardner, Frieda Lawrence, Sinclair Lewis, Percy Marks, Upton Sinclair, John Steinbeck, Carl Van Vechten, Thornton Wilder, Edmund Wilson, and Thomas Wolfe. Those are the authors I was then reading.

In the account of some events in this memoir, there are a few discrepancies to be noted with the accounts of others. This is particularly true with regard to the "Rosemary" affair. The young woman involved was disguised as "Gloria Dart" in a diary kept by Mrs. Laura Guthrie Hearne, Fitzgerald's part-time secretary that summer. A portion of Mrs. Hearne's diary appeared in *Esquire* (December 1964). I was mentioned a few times in that portion, but my name was purposely misspelled by editor Arnold Gingrich as another form of disguise.

Mrs. Hearne's account, which I take to be accurate, doesn't agree at all points with what Fitzgerald told me. He always spoke to me of the young woman as "Rosemary." I never met her, though I learned by accident that he wasn't using her right name (which I also learned). He wasn't merely protecting her, for he felt that she resembled the young actress Rosemary in *Tender Is the Night.* With his novelist's passion for making copy out of all experience, Fitzgerald hadn't lied to me about certain events, but had used his poetic imagination and his sense of the dramatic to embroider the details, oh, just a little and to make the story, as he felt, more true than life. So far as possible I have told that story in his own words.

That summer in Asheville everything had crashed about him. He was a physical, emotional, and financial bankrupt. He smoked and drank steadily, but ate very little; he took pills to sleep a few hours, and he could scarcely write what he thought was a decent line. He was a stranger in Asheville and suffered from loneliness in spite of his saying that a writer must have solitude to practice his craft. His visits to our bookshop kept him from feeling completely out of touch with the world of books and writers, and I think they cheered him during some of his loneliest times. When he talked to me I often had the impression that he was not speaking of himself, but of someone else, and that I served him not only as a companion but also as a sounding board for his ideas. But he listened, too; he was interested in learning from me how a young writer survived during the Depression. He also had a passion for teaching. Eleven years older than I was, he seemed eager to guide me into writing honest fiction rather than to see me become a press agent or take to thinking in terms of proletarian platitudes.

Trying to guide me was an expression of his faith in youthful talent, its spirit and ideals. Fitzgerald honestly believed that it was impossible to write without hope and that the young possessed hope in abundance. Having experienced "the intensity of art," he felt that nothing else that happened to him could ever mean so much as the sense of being completely absorbed in the creative process. Once he showed me a clipping in which Rockwell Kent, the artist, author, and outspoken radical, was quoted as saying, "I think that the ideals of youth are fine, clear and unencumbered, and that the real art of living consists in keeping alive the conscience and sense of values that we once had when we were young." Fitzgerald practiced that real art not only in his work but also to some extent in his life, disorderly as it was. He kept alive to the end the conscience and values of his youth.

Acknowledgments

Iowe a great debt to Mrs. Laura Guthrie Hearne, with whom I have been corresponding and sharing memories of Fitzgerald for more than a decade, and to Lottie, whose name I have changed; to the late William C. Weber of Scribners and Harrison Smith of *The Saturday Review of Literature;* and to Dr. William H. Davis, now practicing in southern California. I am indebted to Malcolm Cowley for his critical and factual assistance in preparing this manuscript for publication; to Professor Matthew J. Bruccoli, editor of the *Fitzgerald/Hemingway Annual,* for critical and factual suggestions; to Mrs. Ellen Prescott Davidson for editorial and helpful advice during its preparation; and to Monica Hannasch for her suggestions and encouragement while writing the book.

Biographies and studies of Fitzgerald and other books which proved invaluable for background material include works by Arthur Mizener, H. D. Piper, Robert Sklar, and the late Andrew Turnbull, besides *The Moveable Feast* by Ernest Hemingway, *Exile's Return* by Malcolm Cowley, *The Great Tradition* by Granville Hicks, *The Hollow Men* by Michael Gold, *The Decline of the West* by Oswald Spengler, *The American Jitters* by Edmund Wilson, *The Creative Process* edited by Brewster Ghiselin, *The Fitzgerald/Hemingway Annual* edited by Matthew J. Bruccoli, and *The Crack-up,* the Fitzgerald collection edited by Edmund Wilson. The Fitzgerald letters, edited by Turnbull, were helpful in rounding out episodes and evoking Fitzgerald's speech, which often sounded as though he were dictating to a secretary.

I am grateful to the following for additional information, assistance, and encouragement: Millen Brand, Milena and V. J. Buttitta, Carvel Collins, Jonathan Daniels, Charles W. Dibbell, Lawrence Gellert, Arnold Gingrich, Paul Green, Granville Hicks, William Hogan, Hobe

Morrison, Anna and Peter Neagoe, Luther Nichols, Eleanor Pinkham, Frances Steloff, Ruth and John Vassos, Frances Winwar, Ken Wong, and Alan D. Williams of The Viking Press.

The Lost Summer

1

Asheville in the summer of 1935. At the time my wife and I had a small bookshop there in the lower arcade of the George Vanderbilt Hotel. It wasn't a profitable venture, though it was next door to a thriving beauty salon, but I earned some bread by writing newspaper articles and by acting as publicity man for the North Carolina Symphony Orchestra. Of course I was writing a novel—two novels, as a matter of fact—and I often worked on them after the shop was closed.

That Saturday night I was at the typewriter, as I usually was for a couple of hours after supper. A lone saxophone wail and the shuffle of dancing feet filtered down from the hotel ballroom. There was a tapping on the glass wall behind me. The door was shut, the rapping sounded far away. I absently turned to see who was there.

Near the glass door stood a slight, blondish, collegiate-looking chap, apparently of the Asheville summer social crowd, hatless and casual in his gray flannels and light tweed jacket. He was making frantic signals as he pointed down the white marble steps. I rose and opened the door.

"Where's the men's room?"

"Downstairs," I snapped.

Whenever there was a dance, guests strayed down the arcade and tapped on the shop's wall, scouting for a bottle, a hotly needed contraceptive, or a vanished date, but rarely to rent or buy a book. If by chance talk got around to books, it was invariably about such best-sellers as *Anthony Adverse*, the first of those long romantic novels that promised an escape from the Depression.

"It's locked," the visitor said, as though expecting me to produce the key.

I went down the stairs to look. I had never done that before, but his voice had a quality that I responded to. He was right, the double door was shut. I checked my wrist watch as I came back up. He was standing by the door of the shop, smoking and wavering a bit, more from absorption in himself, it seemed to me, than from the effect of booze. His face was drawn, pale, and gloomy, the overhead light making it look like a detachable mask.

"They lock it at eleven."

"My God. What's the time?"

"Almost midnight."

"Why the curfew?" he grimaced. "I've been drinking beer. A lot of it."

"There's one up the hall." I pointed toward the staircase. "Off the ballroom."

"Bases loaded." He looked at me. "You have no key?"

"No."

"Where do you go—after hours?"

I smiled. "A garden wall."

"Show me."

He followed me through the half-lit shop. Most of the illumination spilled in from the arcade. I opened the front door between the window displays. He stepped out on the sidewalk.

"To the left." I walked behind him in the moonlit narrow side-street. "Might be muddy after that cloudburst at supper time."

He mumbled and advanced, a bit unsteady but light on his feet. We reached the arched gate at the back of the hotel. I unlatched it and led him under a dripping pergola. The scent of wisteria, cape jasmine, mimosa, and overripe magnolias honeyed the Carolina night. We cut across flowering shrubs and bushes, a mass of gladiolus, and honey-suckle climbing up the side of the wall. The garden was drenched in moonlight. My favored spot was hidden from view by a giant hydrangea blooming in the soft light like a bunch of circus balloons. I made an after-you-Alphonse gesture.

"I'm on the wagon," he murmured when I joined him off to the side. "No hard liquor. Only beer. When I swell up I switch to cokes."

Curiously, this was the moment I recognized him. The well-shaped head, the high brow, straight nose, full mouth, and slightly jutting chin. Against the glow of a lamp, the silhouette formed a romantic profile—sensitive, handsome, and youthful like that of a juvenile star. I had seen it before.

"You're Scott Fitzgerald."

He glanced at me in surprise, then stepped back into the shadow.

"You could tell?"

It wasn't really a question but a statement, a self-directed irony. Symbol and historian of the Jazz Age, he was now a memory more than he was a living person. His college boys and flappers were already a thing of the past when I had read about them at the university, the stories re-creating an era, like a sentimental song, of tea dances at the Plaza, of proms and wild bootleg drinking parties. The corsages were long faded, the flapper trimmings stored in the attic, and the musicians weren't playing "Poor Butterfly" in two-step but "Brother, Can You Spare a Dime?"

"Your profile's as famous as John Barrymore's," I said falsely.

"John's profile," he said, walking away from the wall, "is a romantic symbol."

"Yours means more to me." I stopped after catching a look from him. I had only wanted to say that his novels meant a great deal to me. What I didn't intend to say was that the legend of Scott and Zelda Fitzgerald was vivid to me still. "I know your profile from that photo in *Living Authors*. I see it like a silhouette. That's how I recognized you."

"I look that different now?"

"No, not at all." I noticed my mistake. "I didn't see your profile till now."

"I know the photo. Better than most of those masks and chromos of me in newspaper morgues and my publisher's files." He walked up the path briskly, lifting himself from his gloom, and turned back after a silence. "Who are you?"

"Nobody. Tony Buttitta."

"Sounds Italian. I hated Italians once. Jews too. Most foreigners. Mostly my fault like everything else. Now I only hate myself."

"I hated Anglo-Saxon Bible Belt Protestants once," I rejoined. "Irish Catholics too."

"For good reasons, I bet."

"I suppose. I got over it and don't hate myself."

"Tony." He eyed me from a distance. "Don't call yourself nobody—unless that's all you are. Your bookshop?"

"My wife runs it." I nodded. "I do freelance writing and things."

He walked across the softly lit garden.

"Moonlight is vastly overrated," he mused, waiting for me to latch the gate. "What kind of writing?"

I told him that I wrote book reviews, features, and interviews for newspapers, and was learning publicity from the conductor of the

North Carolina Symphony Orchestra, which was summering there.

"No fiction?"

"Starting a second novel."

"And the first?"

"Making the rounds."

"Writing and publicity make a lousy gin rickey." He frowned and walked toward the hotel. "I tried stories while giving my best to advertising once. The stuff was forced, thin and trashy—with a dash of smart writing. I sold one out of a hundred, the rest bounced back. I kissed the job good-by and went back to my novel with everything I had. A novel never takes less."

We stopped before the shop as he lit a cigarette. The book display caught his eye. He asked whether the hotel was a good location; I replied that it was fair and the rent low even for Depression times. Mostly the customers were women reading best-sellers and purple-passion thrillers like *Impatient Virgin* and *Naked on Roller Skates*. He looked over the titles; I went inside and flipped the switch, flooding the books with light.

"You have my latest," he said, entering. The gloomy mask vanished, his cheeks were taking on color. He advanced to the window, reached for the copy of *Taps at Reveille*, and turned the pages. "First copy I've seen in weeks. How is it going?"

"Sold two or three," I lied.

"Going slow everywhere. Reviews mostly indifferent. I sweated picking the stories and rewriting some—got into a hellish stew. It has one of my top stories."

" 'Babylon Revisited,' " I said quickly.

"You liked it?" He spoke as though my opinion could mean something to him.

"Very much. I put it with the best of Hemingway and Faulkner." I went to the shelf behind the desk. "I reviewed it for a couple of Carolina papers."

"I must've seen one," he said, after a moment's thought. "I believe Scribners sent it to me. I don't remember that it was signed."

"I initial some reviews."

I took down a scrapbook and showed him the review. He said it was the one. I found the other; he seemed pleased that I had mentioned Hemingway and Faulkner in it. As I put back the file he strolled over to the fiction shelf. Out came a Modern Library copy of *The Great Gatsby*.

"All you have of mine?"

"All I can get," I said. *"Tender Is the Night* seems out of stock, out of print, or something. I've ordered it for a couple of psychiatrists here."

"Bennett Cerf ought to put it in the Modern Library too," he said, pleased. "Don't you think it ought to go well?"

"Yes. I'll drop him a note."

"You know Bennett?"

"In a business way. I wish I had a copy," I added. "I'd like to read it again."

"Took nine years and all my innards."

"I think it's your most profound novel."

"A novelist's novel," he said with an ironic grin. "Not glossy and entertaining like *Private Worlds."*

"Authors like that are slick, rental library, book-of-the-monthers," I remarked, ignoring the fact that he had been a pillar of *The Saturday Evening Post.*

"Hollywood was interested until that one came along. I was banking on a movie sale to get out of a hole."

"You know Hollywood better than I do."

"At least you keep me in the best company. Not Lewis, Dell, or Steinbeck. But between Faulkner and Flaubert and close to Hemingway."

"That shelf's by authors—alphabetical."

"Thank you, father." He patted the copy of *The Great Gatsby* and put it back. "I don't see any Farrell."

"I sold the last *Studs* yesterday."

"Don't put him near me. He's a phony like Steinbeck."

"Okay," I said to humor him.

"Any Lardner?"

"Not at the moment."

"One of our greatest humorists since Mark Twain. And like Joyce he created a language of his own—in a popular American idiom."

He picked up *Taps at Reveille* again. "Your pen."

Fitzgerald held out his hand. It was large for a man his size, white and a bit shaky. I reached for a pen and gave it to him. He sat at the desk, opened the book at the flyleaf, and looked up.

"Your name isn't easy."

I spelled it out for him.

He sprawled in a broad, generous, and jerky childlike hand, "For Tony Buttitta/ from his friend/ Scott Fitzgerald/ Ashville 1935." He left the "e" out of Asheville; I showed it to him. Shaking his head he put a hand on my arm. At that moment we slipped into an intimacy that was to last most of the time I knew him.

"Bunny Wilson calls me the world's worst speller. But maybe Zelda is." He paused at the sound of her name. "I wrote Asheville that way in my first novel. It was Monsignor Darcy's town before Thomas Wolfe changed it to Altamont. I never thought I'd be spending time here."

A dark thought seemed to cross his mind. He flipped the pages to the back, stopped, and picked up a pencil. Then he scribbled something, shut the book, and set it near the typewriter. I didn't read what he wrote until later.

A page of mine was in the machine. He read it aloud: "J. Alexander 'Bull' Durham was built like a bull, he snorted and bellowed like one, and was full of the stuff that bore its name. Big Four Buyers followed him from the Flue-Cured Belt to the prized Golden Leaf Tar Heel Country. The biggest warehouses rumbled with his fall chant: *Hey-ding-dee-day. Dee-dee-do. Ding-dee-do. Ding-dee-day!*"

"A fast opener," he said.

I thanked him but my words were drowned out by the orchestra. It burst into a fast number. The trumpet picked up the tune, the drums beat it wildly, and the low ceiling above our heads throbbed with stomping feet.

"My God!" He grabbed my arm. "I forgot my Dollar Woman. Join us!"

—————————2

Fitzgerald was out of cigarettes. The lobby stand was
shut, so we strolled around to
a store that was still open. As we started back toward the hotel, he
stopped to light a Chesterfield. Across the street near the entrance
stood Lottie, with her twin black poodles, talking to a tall Negro
doorman in uniform. She was in her usual costume: a smart hat,
white kid gloves, and a leather bag slung over her shoulder, while
under her arm she carried a book, the latest best-seller, like a badge of
refinement.

At once Fitzgerald noticed the attractive woman. She was laughing
with a reserve becoming to a lady of the South. Shapely and graceful,
with a mass of curly reddish hair, she had the manner of a spirited
young society matron visiting in the mountain resort. She enjoyed
playing the role. I didn't know who or what Fitzgerald meant by his
Dollar Woman, but I was sure he wasn't referring to Lottie.

One of Asheville's most exclusive harlots, her charms were available
only to guests of the luxury hotels. Lottie needed no pimp, paid off no
police; the poodles were a conversation piece. They picked up her
dates among the wealthy visitors while she promenaded them among
the sunny acres around Grove Arcade and the Battery Park Hotel,
where Mount Pisgah and the Rat loomed above the mist of the Great
Smokies.

Her pets, Juliet and Romeo, were rewarded with studded brass
collars, orange silk bows, French perfume, bits of filet mignon, and
Viennese marzipan. Though Lottie rarely opened a book, her custom
of carrying one somehow enhanced that air of chic and respectability
which deceived the most observing eye. Fitzgerald, good at sizing up
people, was no exception.

"I've seen her somewhere," he said, wondering where she belonged

9

in his extravagant years. "She reminds me of Katharine Hepburn."

"She's a damned good actress," I quickly said, "but no Hepburn."

"I always get a lift from a pretty woman—if she has style. Who is she?"

I hated to disillusion him.

"My God!"

I remember the scorn in his voice and his gesture—tossing his half-smoked cigarette away in disgust. He had taken her for a theatrical or social figure he might have known in Southern Pines, Old Westbury, or on the Riviera.

"Lottie fooled me too," I assured him, wanting to soften the insult to his acumen. "The day I met her, she strolled in behind Betty Bronson, the girl who played *Peter Pan* in the movies. There wasn't anything less distinctive about Lottie. I like her better than most of the society women."

The yelp of a poodle rose on the night air above the strains of ballroom music. His thoughts miles away from his Dollar Woman, Fitzgerald stood across the street to observe Lottie further, motivated as a writer now that he wasn't interested in her personally. She was talking to her pets in a soothing voice while the smiling doorman was down on his haunches stroking both so that neither would start another jealous burst of howling.

Fitzgerald was again shocked when I told him that Lottie had once asked my wife if she would like to join her on a dinner date with "two nice friends" from Long Beach, California. Lottie had taken a fancy to us; she knew business was slow and that Remy loved to dance. We laughed it off, as no offense was intended despite the implication.

"No offense!" He glared at me as though I weren't worthy of the inscription he had written in *Taps at Reveille* and was about to go back and rip out the flyleaf.

"Hold your horses," I said. Interested as he was in debutantes and wealthy people, there were nevertheless things he didn't know about them. "Lottie never double-dates with other harlots, but with pretty society women who are fed up with tennis, honeymoon bridge, and eighteen-hole golf. She picks them up at the country club, the smartest parties, Grove Park Inn—"

"I live there!" A scandalized tone, yet he turned to look at Lottie with renewed interest.

"That's where she dines with her society extras. Lottie told me about a couple of them. One said she'd donate the tip she got to her favorite charity, and the other was set to stay for the final act. Lottie sent her away. She says amateur competition is the worst kind."

"You mean she . . ." He was still looking at her.

"The men flip a coin to see who's first. The loser has a couple of brandies till it's his turn."

A long dark limousine rolled up and stopped before the hotel. The Negro rushed to open the door, the poodles yelped and hopped in together, and Lottie, graciously casual, followed. As the car sped off in the moonlight, the doorman went inside and we crossed the street.

"A late, all-night date," I said. "If it's amusing she may tell me about it."

"Is that buck her pimp?"

"No," I said sharply. He still didn't understand about Lottie. And he had betrayed another lack of understanding that was to show itself later on.

Fitzgerald and I pushed through the hotel lobby buzzing with lanky, pink-cheeked youths in black ties and their dates frothy in mauve and turquoise. At the ballroom door he stopped, looking for his table.

Tall potted plants and velvet-draped windows spaced the walls evenly, crystal chandeliers glittered in patterns above, although the vast room was in semidarkness. Baby spots flooded the bandstand at the far end where the white-jacketed leader stood rushing his men through "Ain't She Sweet." The dancers whirled, shivered, and swayed with the frenzy of the twenties when the Charleston was new and Fitzgerald was a sad young man. In one of his bitter moods later, he said: "I'll be forty next year, if I'm unlucky enough to make it. I should have gone at thirty. When I was at the very top."

He ignored the youthful abandon of the dancers as though he had never been a part of it, and led me up a crowded row of tables lit by small, shaded lamps. A woman's voice, firm but soft, called his name in the darkness. He stopped and held out his hand toward a shadowy figure.

"Scott, I thought you got lost," she said in a concerned tone.

"It's Tony's fault." And to me, he said, "This is my Dollar Woman." He then forced me into his chair, gesturing to a passing waiter to bring another. "I call her that because she charged me a dollar to hold my hand."

"Scott—"

He waved aside her prim objection. I'm sure he introduced her as Mrs. Laura Guthrie. I couldn't recall it years later; for a quarter century she remained fixed in my memory as Scott's Dollar Woman. The waiter brought the chair. Fitzgerald sat between us, his back to the revelry on the dance floor.

"She's my mistress." He winked at me, as if to scandalize her. "She belongs to anybody for a dollar. Not her body—her hand. Must be thirty, forty, fifty, don't you think?"

I remember Laura as pretty, bright, and rather proper, an attractive divorcee who seemed not to mind how old she was or what he said about her. I had the impression that she was his secretary, companion, nurse, anything but a romance. There was no mistaking her. Laura was no social butterfly, no Lottie playing a role; she was a lady, firm in her gentility in a world going fast the other way.

"What's your drink?"

"Beer."

"I'm on beer." He stopped a waiter to order three bottles. "My old friends don't believe me. They say I always boast about being on the wagon. This time it's true, isn't it?"

His Dollar Woman was studying me to see what he had picked up this time: a college chum, perhaps someone who might exploit him, or a new bar companion. He must have noticed it, as he now explained who I was, and how we had met in the lower arcade and gone to the garden. I smiled at her and in the dim light noticed her penetrating eyes, ladylike complexion, and the dark evening gown she was wearing for the occasion.

"Sometime I want to see that garden by daylight," he said.

"An old lady's hobby," I ventured. "Like any other. Night gives it that special look."

"Night lends enchantment to everything."

"It does something for a title too."

"I owe it to Keats. He saved me at the last minute. But I had thought about it before. Scribners didn't like it. I forced it on them." He turned to her. "Tony's writing a novel. Maybe he'll tell us about it."

The waiter showed up with a tray of bottles and filled our glasses. I picked up mine, hoping we would forget the novel, but Fitzgerald mentioned it again. I plunged ahead to please him and to keep the conversation going. I should have told them about *Bull Durham*, the novel he had seen a page of in the typewriter, instead of *No Resurrection*.

"A college novel set in Chapel Hill. The hero's a Negro who imitates the worst in whites to become a big shot—a kind of superman. He sells his body to a med student. A prof's wife encourages him to try and get it back—to save his soul. She is childless, sees him as her saviour, and brings about his destruction. A black and white Faust— you might say."

The woman was silently horrified. Fitzgerald frowned on a Negro hero but was intrigued by the variation on the idea of a man destroying himself to regain his soul. He reached for his glass and went on smoking; she wisely changed the subject and I was grateful to her.

Suddenly he said, "Be a good girl and read Tony's hand. Reading hands is her hobby. She knows her stuff and will tell you. I'll see that this is on the house."

"Of course I'll read your friend's hand," she said in her forceful voice. "You know I only charge at Inn parties and conventions."

"You forced me to cross your palm with silver," he teased, "like a shrewd carnival gypsy."

"And you called yourself Mr. Johnson!" she said with a little laugh. "I thought you were with that hair dressers' convention at first—you were so well groomed."

"My God!" He grimaced and covered his face, as though she had put him in his place. "She saw through my incognito and got me down pat. Now I want to see her work on you."

She leaned forward and took my hands. The light was hazy, Fitzgerald struck matches from his packet so she could see the lines. I don't know what she saw but she decided I was no menace and gave me a pleasant smile. We ceased being three strangers; and, as she spoke, she revealed herself as a compassionate and unforgettable woman. Ten years ago I learned from Professor Matthew J. Bruccoli that Laura Guthrie Hearne was still in Asheville; we started corresponding and sharing our memories of Fitzgerald and she gave me permission to quote from her letters. She passed away in the fall of 1973.

"Look at his thumbs," Scott said with the excitement of discovery. But she went on examining the hands silently.

"What do you see?" he asked impatiently. He was frankly curious; later he told me that he believed in palmistry, Zelda too, as the hand was an extension of the human mind and personality.

"They're unusual, Scott," she finally said, running her index finger over my palms. "You have a varied life. Business and the arts. Money will come easily though you're having a hard time now. You're intuitive—like Scott. You also have a rare line. Combined head and heart. I believe it's the . . . Napoleon line. It denotes vitality and . . ."

Fitzgerald said Napoleon was one of his heroes, and wanted to

know more about the line and why it was named after him. She ignored him and went on checking the mounds, fingers, thumb spread,
and various configurations which are telling in an individual.

I understood what she was doing. I had learned to read hands from
a gypsy at whose tent I spieled when I worked in a circus. Even if his
Dollar Woman was an amateur, she didn't strike me as a dabbler who
read hands parlor-fashion. The gypsy, too, had commented on the
combined head and heart line, but had given it no name.

"You have a flair for words," she resumed. "You will write a lot.
Mostly trash. But you won't do anything serious until you write
about yourself and . . ."

Fitzgerald was no longer with us. We lost him and the matches
when the musicians slid into a medley of Jerome Kern's songs from
Show Boat, *Sally*, and *Roberta*. He faced the bandstand and sang in a
toneless voice, forgetting us and the dancers in the shadowed
ballroom, and then the words of "Lovely to Look At" softly to himself—faraway, and open to all the melancholy of his memories. Laura
turned to him solicitously, spoke his name. His face, profile to us and
cupped in one hand, bore an expression that seemed close to tears.
She didn't persist; her tact and sensitivity were clearly the basis of
their relationship.

"You'll have trouble with love and the success you want and need,"
she said in a half-whisper. "Neither will come easily. But with your
talent and vitality you . . ."

Fitzgerald lit a cigarette and faced us without really seeing us. She
finished the reading. I mumbled thanks, bid them good-by, and left
the ballroom. I was affected more by his toneless lament than by what
she had seen in my hand.

The moon was high. The streets mirrored its silver light. I walked
up College Street, turned in on Spruce, and stopped in front of the
rooming house still owned by Thomas Wolfe's mother, the Old Kentucky Home—the Dixieland of *Look Homeward, Angel*. I had slept in
one of its dingy rooms, perhaps in Wolfe's iron-framed bed, before
moving to an apartment house nearby. Whenever I passed the weathered old structure, its gables and rambling porches, I often thought of
the troubled Gants and imagined hearing querulous voices.

Wolfe had been my reason for coming to Asheville that summer
with the orchestra. He wasn't in town; I was never to meet him. I had
no idea that Fitzgerald was there—even if he had misspelled the name
Asheville in his first novel. Standing in the silvered street, I remembered his words: "Moonlight is vastly overrated," "Night lends en-

chantment to everything." It was a troubled world for famous authors along with the rest of us that summer of 1935.

Sunday morning, still under the spell of that night's encounter, I went to the bookshop. I picked up *Taps at Reveille*, read the short inscription, and studied his handwriting. I went over in my mind everything that happened and noted it on the flyleaves of *Living Authors*.

3

That summer I got the impression that Fitzgerald desperately needed friends. He was a stranger in Asheville, though he spoke of Lefty and Nora Flynn of Tryon, a resort about fifty miles away. I was to learn later that most of his old friends were fed up with his truculent moods, his college-boy antics when he lost control, and his awe of the leisurely rich. Hemingway had called him a "rummy" and had lost respect for him as a serious writer. His Princeton chum John Peale Bishop said in a magazine piece that he was a social climber. His editor at Scribners, Maxwell Perkins, and his agent, Harold Ober, faithful friends to whom he owed thousands, didn't think he could quit drinking or go back to writing. They were all convinced that he was an alcoholic in need of a cure.

Despite the role of liquor in shattering Zelda's life and wrecking his own, Fitzgerald told me that it was a writer's curse—"the fatal flaw" in his own makeup—and cited famous names to prove it, noting with mocking satisfaction those it had destroyed. It amused him to say that drinking came naturally to him; he sprang from a people whose love of the bottle was part of their charm. And though he was aware that he used the very real pressures of his life as an excuse for drink, he was stubborn about quitting. He made occasional attempts to ration himself that smacked of self-denial and atonement, switched to wine and beer, and then to Cokes and sweets.

He often spoke of his daughter Scottie, who was away at camp or with friends, and of Zelda, who was being treated for schizophrenia in a Baltimore clinic. He blamed himself for her breakdown and the consequent separation, and longed for the good gay times they had once shared. Deserted by old friends and reaching out for strangers, unknown to the new generation and neglected by his own—as he lamented—Fitzgerald was at times a warm, lovable, self-confident and stimulating companion, occasionally posing as the oracle of his age. At other times he was a schoolboy whose silences, rages, and maudlin outbursts were a plea for help and for reassurance of his personal and literary worth.

Often when I saw him he cried, suddenly, as if he were an overwrought, indulged child. All he needed was to hear some romantic line spoken in a film, or a melody he had danced to or heard in a Broadway musical show. All he had to see was a pair of frilly slippers in a shop window or young lovers holding hands. His eyes would fill, a hand shielding his face, and the tears fell. Though momentarily purged and restored when he wiped his pale blue eyes, he felt ashamed and swore.

"God, I'm a lousy weakling!" His tone at such times was scornful, helpless, and yet defiant. "I've tried to be tough and hard-boiled. It's no use. It's an act. I've been acting all my life. But I always go to pieces. I can't make it stick. I hate myself—an unbearable son of a bitch. How can you listen!"

Once started, Fitzgerald couldn't stop. His monologues were full of self-pity. "Life ended when Zelda and I smashed. The cards began falling badly for us early. Everything went to pieces and it's a long uphill pull now. It's harder when you're past thirty. My God, how I miss my youth! Life hasn't much to offer but youth. What a fund of hope I had then. I raised hell and whooped it up. Got roaring drunk. I cry easily. I'm losing my grip, get the horrors when I'm alone. I dread most the years ahead.

"My God, nobody's reading me now! For ten years I turned out happy-ending stuff under the whip of the big advertisers. I've lost the knack and the gay parade's passed me by. But I resent those friends who tried to bury me before I was cold. I was a romantic once. I'm a skeptic now. A cynic too. Yes, I'm mature at last—now that I know that's all I ever was—a failure!"

I was to learn later that every time he emerged from a disastrous binge, a relation with a woman, a family crisis, or a lost struggle to write a story, he sang out this claim that he was mature at last.

"You're mature and I'm damned sure you're no failure," I said one sunny afternoon as we strolled toward Beaucatcher Mountain on the outskirts of town. "You're one of the four or five top American writers—and you don't have to hatch a book a year to prove it."

He stopped suddenly and gave me a sharp look.

"Who are the others?"

"Friends of yours. One's a friend of mine," I replied. "Hemingway, Faulkner, and it's a tossup between Wolfe and Dos Passos."

"I'm fed up with Wolfe's great love affair with the universe. His sprawling style, too. You think he's tops."

"I went to Chapel Hill. He's a legend there," I said. "The way you must be at Princeton."

"A hell of a reason. You know Faulkner?"

"Yes."

But I was curious to learn why he had come to what the Asheville Chamber of Commerce proudly advertised as "The Land of the Sky."

"Whatever you're thinking, it's probably wrong."

It was a reference to his drinking. Later I learned from books about Fitzgerald that the previous winter had been a depressing one for him. The job of seeing *Taps at Reveille* through publication, after the disappointment of *Tender Is the Night* the year before, had left him exhausted in body and spirit. He had been depressed by the tepid reception of the novel; debts had piled up, Zelda's case appeared hopeless, and he was unable to write. Drink had helped to keep him going, but not to pull him out of his wretched state.

On an impulse in February Fitzgerald had hopped into his old car and driven south alone—to take inventory of himself and to find a workable future. Greeted by blossoming dogwood at Hendersonville, a small resort near Asheville, he stopped there. He told me how he had shacked in a dollar room, washed his own socks, and survived on fruit, beer, and dime tins of potted meat—the forerunner of canned dog food. His funds were low, but they did all right at the Skyland Hotel. Living alone was a good restorative, he said, even if it left him time for brooding.

"You know the Skyland?"

"Yes, and Old Gaunt, that unfinished hulk of a skyscraper the promoters left shipwrecked in the middle of nowhere. One of the relics of the Boom-and-Bust."

"Those windows are like giant loopholes. They haunted me at first with their emptiness. Sickness and poverty are a wretched combination. And poverty is one of the unforgivable things in life."

Fitzgerald ventured to nearby Tryon to see the Flynns, a charming couple like the Murphys he had known on the Riviera in the twenties. The Flynns adopted him as the Murphys had done in those happy days with Zelda; they invited him to drop in whenever he wished. Nora was a sister of Lady Astor, Lefty a former college athlete and adventurer; she was a Christian Scientist and tried to get Fitzgerald to become one to help control his drinking—as she herself had done. He saw them off and on, and met their social and literary crowd before going back North.

He had come back to Asheville in May for a cure. It wasn't the kind his friends had prescribed, he told me, though there was such an establishment in Asheville. We both knew about Kenilworth Inn, a castlelike retreat for alcoholics whose wealthy families could afford to keep them there. The cure consisted of a five-day period of drying out, rationing, and abstinence. But the inmates had their weekends when they were free to indulge in another spree. Kenilworth Inn was supervised by a medical staff and proved successful, he said, for the management.

Before I came to Asheville my friend Bill Davis, a Chapel Hill med student, had told me that the mountain town was also known as "America's Magic Mountain," after the Thomas Mann novel, for the treatment of pulmonary ailments. Almost a mile high, it is surrounded by the Great Smokies and the Blue Ridge Mountains. Fitzgerald said he was sent there because of a recurrence of his long-dormant tuberculosis. His beloved Keats had succumbed to it in his twenties. From what I later learned the disease was more romantic and imaginary than real, and Fitzgerald had at times used it as a cover-up for personal disaster, failure, or excessive drinking.

This flare-up had grown out of a severe flu attack following his return to Baltimore. According to Fitzgerald's biographers, his doctor put him in Johns Hopkins. And when X-rays revealed a possible lung spot or cavity, he was sent to a noted specialist in Asheville, with the warning that he would be dead within a year if he didn't take care of himself. The specialist was Dr. Paul Ringer, who, as quoted by Fitzgerald, repeated the warning, which he stoically accepted as his "grave sentence." While being treated Fitzgerald was allowed to stay at Grove Park Inn, the resort hotel, because he had convinced the doctor that news of his illness might leak out if he were in the hospital, and this might endanger his earnings as a writer.

"When you write your New York friends, don't mention I am here or why. We know some of the same people. It would get around that I'm laid up. I told Max Perkins about it. He's one person up there I can trust."

At the time his Dollar Woman was also one of Dr. Ringer's patients. She recently wrote me not to repeat the story that Fitzgerald had tuberculosis. She said that her doctor referred to it as a "myth." I quote from her letter: "Scott clung to the illusion that he could convince people that he had it—even Dr. Ringer. But the doctor was disgusted with the hoax and told me so. . . . After all, it was Scott's heart that failed. Tuberculosis did not kill him."

I later learned the cure was simple: rest, no liquor, solid food, and flattering attention from doctors, nurses, secretaries, maids, and waiters—which he seemed to need more and more as his friends dropped away. Fitzgerald was soon pronounced out of danger. Instead of thanking the gods or his strong recuperative powers, Fitzgerald said that he suddenly cracked.

This puzzled me, I remember, but he explained that when the doctors had given him what he took to be a death sentence, he hadn't shed a tear. Fate had stepped in to take over his affairs. His only concern was for Zelda and Scottie. Once he had looked after them, he was lulled by the feeling that he was free of all responsibilities and had only to wait for the end—his deliverance.

"When I got the good news, it meant the big scene was off. I felt sorry for myself and cried. I had to face the whole damned mess all over again and I didn't have it in me. I couldn't pull myself together for another push. All my reserves were gone. It was as simple as the law of gravity. I collapsed."

His slightly bloodshot eyes, shaky white hands, and the thick sound of his voice—all from too much gin—didn't add up to a picture of someone having a breakdown, in my limited view then. I was eleven years younger than Fitzgerald.

"When did you get over it?"

"I haven't—yet."

As we started back toward town, Fitzgerald assured me that he was no hypochondriac reveling in imaginary ailments for the sake of attention. Yet even then he was certain that his old cirrhosis of the liver was plaguing him. Insomnia had a firm hold on him; he was taking a combination of pills to get a few hours' sleep. He took benzedrine (years before bennies became fashionable) to wake up in the morning so he could think and try to write. He needed a drink to stir his memory, heighten emotions and thoughts, and give his style brilliance. If he took one drink too many, he couldn't think or write, and another day was shot.

"Insomnia goes with alcohol, and some of my doctors encouraged me to have a nightcap."

Health and money were a man's first considerations, he said as we strolled back. He was quoting Samuel Butler, one of his lifelong admirations. But he was now alarmed by what was happening to him as a writer. Though by temperament a serious writer, he spoke of his facility—he called it "cheap"—as an author of slick magazine stories. They had supported him and Zelda in style, but he had abused the talent and it seemed to have vanished. *The Saturday Evening Post* now was rejecting his stories. I later learned that some of the stories he wrote at the time were so lifeless and badly written that other editors were sending them back to his agent.

But now he had also run out of material, he said. His personal experiences had served him well for years; he had used them over and over again, and he needed a new source. His need was so desperate that, as I later read, he had bought the rights to others' personal narratives which showed possibilities. But as a writer whose imagination responded best to his own experiences, he was wasting money and was ashamed of the lackluster stories when they appeared in print.

In his miserable state there was one stimulating thing, he confided as our walk ended and we found ourselves back on Pack Square. (Bill Davis had dubbed it "Sputum Square" because of the tuberculars who came to Asheville for the cure. Some sat on benches under a hotel canopy; across the street one of the town's first skyscrapers stood on the site where Wolfe's father had had his tombstone shop.) Fitzgerald spoke of a wealthy young woman from Memphis; she was staying at the Inn, had recognized him, and had apparently fallen in love with him. She followed him, put herself in his way, and then he found her reading *The Great Gatsby* in the writing room. He admitted being attracted to her.

There was nothing unusual about women's falling for Fitzgerald, seeking romance, adventure, or, more specifically, the privilege of shining in his glory. He was continually meeting women who were impressed by his fame and his gifted understanding—in his writings—of the feminine psyche and the love relationship. Two or three women had wanted to have a child by him that might inherit his writing talent. The woman from Memphis, according to his Dollar Woman, was one of them.

The women who pursued him were rich, young, and sometimes beautiful, he said; but, except for certain brief encounters, they were disappointing because his romantic imagination was still involved with his one great passion, Zelda. Fitzgerald told me he had recently passed up several "gorgeous" opportunities. There was a young society woman who had bribed a bellhop to let her into his suite in a hotel. She was stark naked in his bed when he walked into his room.

"I poured myself a stiff drink and asked her if she weren't ashamed of herself. She said, no, she loved me, though she had never set eyes on me before. She had fallen in love with me from my novels and my picture. I sat on the edge of the bed while she put on her clothes and lectured her on the wide gap between the man and the writer, reality and romance, and told her to fall in love with somebody real instead of a ghost. Then I politely showed her to the door.

"She was a pretty thing and bright, too, but I have known my share of baby vamps, sirens, and brazen women. This Memphis beauty is a thoroughbred like one of her horses. Yes, she owns a stable. She has everything—including one husband, one child. My God! Her grandpa owned half of the town where she lives.

"When I found her reading *Gatsby*, the morning was shot for work. I had taken that drink too many, although I didn't show it. I lifted the book out of her hand and said, 'Silly wasting time on it—with the original around.' I've seen her twice since and . . . I'm the one who's stalling. She's here with an ailing sister. Nerves and something else."

Fitzgerald saw a cab in the square, waved to the driver, took my hand, and left me to ponder his dilemma: "Christ, in my wretched state, she's all I need, don't you think?"

4

I had come to Asheville in the spring. Thomas Wolfe was the reason. In Chapel Hill, where I had spent three years, it was impossible for a hopeful writer not to come under the shadow of the Wolfe legend. It was a vast cloud that mushroomed over the campus in the fall of 1929, when I arrived there from the University of Texas, and it spread so that I can't remember any mention of the Depression until some months later.

Wolfe's first novel, *Look Homeward, Angel*, was discussed in all-night bull sessions everywhere from the hallowed old quadrangle to the new, in literature and drama classes, and particularly at the Carolina Playmakers, which I immediately joined. There, after writing a one-act folk play, *The Return of Buck Gavin*, Wolfe had been advised to switch to the novel. Our password at the time was, "A stone, a leaf, a door," the key words in *Look Homeward*. Almost everyone who had known Wolfe spoke of his gargantuan size, of his words pouring out in a torrent, and thus kept alive the legend of the hillbilly genius from the mountains.

Like many hopefuls who joined the Playmakers to write plays, I longed to go to Asheville and see the family and town he had immortalized in the novel, as a kind of literary pilgrimage. I was unable to go until the spring of 1935, shortly after reviewing *Of Time and the River* for Carolina newspapers. Reading the long book between chores as a United Press reporter in Durham and helping Remy my wife in our bookshop there, I was again under the Wolfe spell. The longing to go to the hills was rekindled with a fervor that insisted it was now or never. So when I was offered the North Carolina Symphony job, though we were doing fairly well in the shop and our Duke University clientele was growing, I accepted it solely because the orchestra was to summer in Asheville.

Of course, I had to stay at the Old Kentucky Home, where much of the first novel takes place, but after a few nights we moved out. Remy found an apartment on nearby Woodfin Street—the street where Wolfe was born—and I scouted for a bookshop location in the downtown commercial area. My search ended when I walked down the street at the side of the George Vanderbilt Hotel and noticed a small store that obviously had been empty for some time.

As I had explained to Fitzgerald, the shop was centrally situated and the rent was cheap. Across the corridor was that beauty salon, which brought a stream of women to the lower arcade. Our earlier shop in Durham, in the Washington Duke Hotel, had been near such a salon, and we had learned that it was an ideal location. It was convenient for idle women—our most faithful lending-library clients—to pick up and return books when they came downtown to get beautified.

Most of our stock consisted of publishers' remainders, which I got from a New York outlet house. These were often books of literary merit, some by established authors, that hadn't caught on, so that publishers had to sell them at a sacrifice to avoid paying additional storage costs. Some were illustrated classics such as *Candide*, some the erotic type like *Aphrodite* by Pierre Louÿs, a book that had quite a vogue at the time. I used such titles as a "come-on" and advertised them as big bargains, from fifty-nine to ninety-nine cents, while doubling the price of other remainders.

The latest titles came from the books I reviewed for the newspapers. I received space rates for writing a daily and a weekly book column, but chiefly I did the reviews to get the books. Most of them went into the circulating library; we preferred to rent them at three cents a day rather than sell them outright. Once sold, like a share of stock, there was no more income from a book. But we ordered copies on demand and when a title became a hot item we bought extra copies to circulate.

Our rental library consisted mostly of the usual fare—mystery and detective fiction, adventure and Westerns, and sexy thrillers bearing such titles as *Professional Virgin* and *Call Her Savage*. I was kind to such books in my reviews; publishers kept sending them and I stirred up reader interest in them. They were our best source of income and some of them circulated until they were tattered and almost fell apart.

Fitzgerald was curious to know about the operation of the small shop. I told him everything, and it sounded like good raw material for fiction. It also seemed to give him an idea of how a struggling young writer managed to make ends meet in that difficult period. He guessed that my *Taps at Reveille* was the review copy that Scribners had sent me; I explained that it belonged to my personal collection and wasn't for sale or rental, but I could order a copy should a customer want it. When he asked whether I had really sold two or three copies, I didn't lie a second time. He reproached me for not having told him the truth and assured me that he could take it.

The most lucrative crowd that patronized our shop were Remy's customers. They were the town's most elegant homosexuals, eager and sensitive lovers of art and literature, often accompanied by well-heeled older men or "queens" with graying hair and a hothouse tan. Remy had an easy and *simpatico* way with them, served them coffee or tea, and chatted with them as though they all belonged to a sewing circle. Some confided in her, and one once asked her to introduce him to a customer, whom he described as a "handsome young man who, unfortunately, was normal as hell." It had been the same at the shop in Durham, but here too the gay set joined our rental library and bought both literary and erotic specials.

"Faggots and whores, like your Lottie," Fitzgerald curtly commented, but this was before he got to know her.

I told him we had other customers, some he might like to meet, bright and socially aware university students spending their vacations in Asheville. He was eventually to meet two of them and join in their discussion, but at the time he wanted to know more about Lottie, even if she was a whore. I can't say whether it was for personal or professional reasons, nor can I remember how much I said to him, yet his questions stand out in my memory.

Yes, I had first met Lottie in the bookshop. She had strolled in with her poodles and we talked about them, not about books. I don't think she had come to rent or buy a book, but before leaving she asked me to give her something light that everybody was talking about. Not for reading, she said with a smile, but for talking about it. At least she was honest, I thought, and without inquiring about her taste, I handed her a Faith Baldwin novel. She gave it back to me, saying she would never read a book written by a woman. I chose a title by Peter B. Kyne or Warwick Deeping. When she returned it a week later Lottie didn't say a word about it; and, after taking out two more books, she admitted that she hadn't opened them; it was just that she liked carrying a book under her arm.

At first I didn't know that Lottie was a professional working with her poodles. I had seen her promenading with them along Grove Arcade as I walked to the symphony office. I didn't have an inkling of how she earned her living until I noticed her chatting—and presumably making dates—with two or three different well-dressed men who casually strolled after her. On one such occasion she and I had been talking near the entrance to the Arcade. She abruptly excused herself when what looked like a middle-aged businessman greeted her; he approached with a friendly nod and tipped his straw with all the respect due a lady.

From that day she took it for granted that I knew and, instead of hiding her profession, she coolly spoke of it as simply a business. But she talked freely with me—not with my wife—and told me amusing tales about some of the classy men she entertained. She preferred the company of men, and though she found Remy pleasant and didn't mind her knowing what she was, Lottie seemed a bit self-conscious in her company. It was just the opposite with the homosexuals, who enjoyed chatting with my wife: they became self-conscious the moment I walked into the shop and changed the subject of their conversation.

Fitzgerald was surprised I couldn't tell him where Lottie lived—in a hotel or a private house. I simply didn't know and made no issue of it when she joined our rental library and gave no address or phone number. She could see that it sounded strange and unbusinesslike, but explained that she was staying with friends and didn't want to bother them with her calls.

Lottie handed me a five-dollar bill instead of the required dollar deposit. I took only a dollar and told her I had sized her up as an honest and responsible woman. It was this gesture, she once told me, that paved the way for our friendship and her confiding to me about her dates and her relations with Fitzgerald later that summer.

The more he learned about Lottie, the more Fitzgerald thought of writing a story about her. But first he had to know the nature of her secret: it was as necessary to him as a key to a lock. He could think up a motive but insisted that the real one would be superior to whatever he might imagine. Were the police after her? How could I be sure the name she gave me—Lottie Stephens—wasn't false? It was common knowledge that prostitutes never operated under their given names.

I admitted he was right and that I was curious too, but I accepted her secret as part of her life. Then I showed him her rental library card. In the blank where I was to have written Lottie's address, I had jotted down at her suggestion "Canine Château"—the place where she left Juliet and Romeo when she couldn't take them on a date.

5

Shortly after our meeting, Fitzgerald told me he had an idea that might make an article for one of the newspapers I wrote for. It was an assessment of the social changes that had taken place in the generations since World War I. He had tried writing it as a magazine piece and given up. I had thought of asking him for an interview, but hesitated because of his past experiences with newsmen. His horror of interviews was known to me; reporters and columnists, annoyed by his early cocky manner and remarks, rarely missed the chance to slap him down—and he knew they had the last word.

When I saw him again he failed to mention the story, and I didn't refer to it. He had dropped by the bookshop and found Remy, whom he had not met before. I was at the symphony office in Grove Arcade. When he learned that Remy was an artist, he became enthusiastic, telling her that art was Zelda's lifelong passion, although she had been sidetracked by writing and ballet, but that she was now back at her easel. The year before there had been an exhibition of her paintings in New York; it had stirred more attention than he had with his last book.

I was typing a publicity release when he walked in the bare office on the ground floor of the Arcade. A book was under his arm; I recognized it by the cover drawing—Ben Hecht's *1001 Afternoons in Chicago*. He waited outside while I finished, pacing the wide, deserted corridors that echoed with every step he took. He was surprised to see only a half-dozen tenants in the building; most of the shops and offices were vacant or hadn't been completed for occupancy. The Arcade was a white elephant and it was typical of the time; the symphony had been donated space there as a cultural organization to help give the impression that prosperity was just around the corner.

The massive edifice squatted on a bulldozed hill. I made a point of telling Fitzgerald that Wolfe had lamented that the hill had lost its graceful contours in the name of progress. The Arcade was one of the two Boom structures—the other being Grove Park Inn—which were built as memorials by E. W. Grove, the patent medicine Chill Tonic King. It had been started on a grander scale than Old Gant in Hendersonville; construction had halted at the fourth floor, making it the worst local calamity of the Crash, except for a couple of sensational suicides. The Crash struck Asheville early, with the collapse of Luke Lea's banking empire, before it reached the proportions of a national catastrophe.

I told Fitzgerald of a land transaction that had become a political scandal, but an amusing one. A short time before land speculation went into a tailspin, a politician bought a plot on the outskirts of Asheville for about five thousands dollars. During the Boom, the property changed hands a dozen times, while its price doubled and tripled with every sale. Its last purchaser was the city; it was to be used as a new cemetery for the fast-growing little metropolis. The first burial was a fiasco—the plot was solid rock. At the time it was referred to as "Mayor Green's Graveyard."

"You didn't tell me your wife was such a pretty brunette. I'd say she looks like Merle Oberon or Hedy Lamarr," Fitzgerald said as we strolled out of the square-block building into the open spaces that faced the Battery Park Hotel.

"Think so?"

"She knows about books and writers. Paints too. You're a lucky feller." He sized me up as though wondering what such a talented beauty saw in one of my short stature and Mediterranean cast—although he was supposed to admire dark hair and eyes over his own light coloring. "She wants to do a silhouette. I told her I'd be glad to pose."

"Sure you want to bother?"

"I've posed before. It's no bother. Where did she get such a pretty French name?"

"She's Irish-French from New Orleans."

That day Fitzgerald was off everything except black coffee and cigarettes. He lit one as we walked to the Battery Park coffee shop and when we sat down he ordered three cups of black coffee. I now noticed that he was edgy and restless; he sighed, fingered the book, and flitted from one thought to another. I wondered why he had come to see me.

"You're probably thinking, what am I doing at Grove Park Inn with the national debt on my back? I'm the American success story. I was born a poor boy and made it in the rich man's world. I'm still a peasant deep down, but I have acquired extravagant tastes. I've been corrupted. I'm hopelessly committed to living beyond my means. A kind of compulsion."

"Of course," I mumbled, and sipped my coffee.

"I'm thinking of Highland Hospital for Zelda. It's a couple of miles from the Inn. Know it?"

"I'll have my friend Bill Davis check it."

"Who's Bill Davis?"

"A med student at Chapel Hill."

"I told you I don't want you to go spreading that I'm here," he said sharply. "Not even as far as Chapel Hill."

"Bill lives here. He's on vacation. His father's in advertising."

The last remark would have been better left unsaid. There was no one like an advertising man to spread news. But it seemed I had reminded him of something and he quickly took it up.

"Advertising—our last frontier. A racket like writing for pictures. I tried it for six months. Big business corrals writers and artists in elegant stables called agencies to glamorize liver pills, deodorants, purgatives, depilatories, and halitosis. They grab the best space to show off their nauseating products and make outlandish promises to a gullible public. Stories and articles are sandwiched between the ads, kicked column by column, page by page, toward the back. You're learning publicity. If you have the knack, your future's in advertising. Read by the millions. The writing of our time."

He then asked if I was serious about writing.

"I think so."

"Then remember that it settles for nothing less than the best. There's no reason for wanting to write unless you're ready to deliver your guts. And you must do it now—while you have youth and vitality. Are you sure?" As I didn't reply, he went on. "Publicity and advertising are sure-fire, like my slick stories. But if you have to write, you know what I am saying. Otherwise you can do better—a hell of a lot better—with this dubious stuff.

"A writer must reflect his world, interpret life, dig out the bare truth. He must have talent and conscience. If he has talent and no conscience, he's a journalist and writes that kind of book. If he has neither, he's a hack. He becomes an advertising man or a press agent. A glorified pimp on the expense account. A serious writer needs a viewpoint of his own—not that of his employer. In a word—character. A rare commodity. Today young people think they can write because they have a story to tell. But it takes more. One also needs a colorful style, besides a point of view. I worked hard to polish my style. Writing itself came easy. Words too. Have you tried poetry?"

"A blues, jazzy kind."

"Makes no difference so long as it comes like a dream from your subconscious. The closing paragraph of one of my best stories is such a song." He paused and spoke in a deep voice I hadn't heard before—the actor's voice. *"Long ago, long ago, there was something in me, but now that thing is gone. Now that thing is gone, that thing is gone. I cannot cry. I cannot care. That thing will come back no more."*

I repeated the refrain and said, "That's a perfect blues."

"It's sentimental. Yes. There was a time when every word struck deep." His voice thickened, he turned his face away. "That something was the love I first brought to Zelda. She refused it. I couldn't afford her. When she said *yes*, I loved her, but not with *that* love. It was gone and never came back."

His nostalgic refrain reminded me of a Joyce poem that Faulkner had recited one night after having taken a drop too many of Carolina corn. It was "Watching the Needleboats at San Sabba," from his collection *Pomes Penyeach*. I remembered only its refrain and that was enough. I thought it might bolster Fitzgerald's morale to learn that Joyce had also indulged in a sentimental moment.

I told him about the poem and then recited the lines: *"No more will the wild wind that passes/ Return, no more return."* It delighted him; he repeated the lines in the same voice he had spoken his own. He excitedly asked whether I had the poem and he could borrow it. I told him it was in my collection and he could have it.

It occurred to me, as he went on, that he hadn't yet said why he had come. The monologue that follows I have reconstructed as faithfully as I could from notes I made on the flyleaves of *Eric Dorn* and *1001 Afternoons in Chicago*. The warm, confident tone of his voice still sounds in my ears after all these years.

"My Dollar Woman finds you unusual—Napoleon line, vitality, intuition, and all. I want to see some of your writing. I wasn't trying to discourage you. I'm a man of many moods. I've thought of chucking it all myself—for the fast buck. I have a cheap streak and could have done it. But I'm too much of a moralist to be satisfied by merely entertaining. I'm so desperate now I would try it—except I've used up everything. I was no seaman like Conrad or London, no doctor like Maugham or Chekhov, no reporter like Ben Hecht or John Reed. I never did anything but live the life I wrote about. Some thought it was gay. I made it seem that way, which is despair turned inside out. Call it a law of style.

"Even if I weren't used up, I don't have to tell you that the trend has changed. This rash of bogus novels about peasants, Holy Roller preachers, millhands, union organizers, strikes—that's the thing. It's due to the Depression. We have lost confidence in our senseless *laissez-faire* economic system. Though I've read Marx, Engels, and company, the workers' world is outside my experience. I was stuck with my own crashes and tried to salvage what I could for my writing. But those bonehead critics have jumped on the proletarian bandwagon. They pile praise on the barnyard boys and dismissed my last two books as trivial and passé."

"You know, fashions in novels change, like everything—if not as often—but you're not passé," I said, wondering if that was what he was getting at. "You're writing about an era that you named and know more about than any other American writer. It's your world as Yoknapatawpha is Faulkner's. You're both literary historians. Most of this other stuff's topical journalism. It'll soon be kicking around musty second-hand bookstores."

But he needed more than assurance, Fitzgerald said, slamming the book on the table. It was a new source of material. He had taken the book from the shop, hoping to find the germ of an idea to stir his tired imagination. Hecht had been a young poet and budding writer with *Eric Dorn;* since exiling himself in Hollywood, as Fitzgerald had done in Europe, Hecht had gone the way of princely extravagances and had come down to the standard product, except for the arty films he was making with their mutual friend Charlie MacArthur. But Hecht, as a newspaperman who worked on a Chicago journal with MacArthur, Carl Sandburg, and Sherwood Anderson, had gathered enough material to last a lifetime.

"It's too late to be a newspaperman, but I was on the tail of an idea last week when I walked into the office of the Tryon weekly. There was a tall, pleasant chap with a young Sandburg face who seemed to be running the works. I pumped him about it and said nothing would please me more than to settle down on such a paper. He knew who I was—we had chatted over coffee at Misseldine's. He gave me a disdainful look as if I were another dude who belonged to the Flynn's flower-and-dog-show crowd.

"At first I resented the look. Then I thought he was probably right. I saw myself, like the rest of my kind, as a soft, flabby, spoiled creature who had never done a day's physical labor. Once I tried, and years ago I thought of going to sea for a couple of years—to make a man of myself. But it's too late for that now. I can't get away from myself or my duty." He held me with his eyes. "I think you might help me."

"How?"

"Probably nothing will come of it, but it's worth a try. From what you told me about your Lottie, the way she operates, her society extras, the poodle pimps, and the men she entertains at the Inn and other places—there might be a story for me. I want to meet her and one of her bored beauties."

"Okay, but I can't promise the beauties."

"Leave that to me. When?"

"Tomorrow—if I see her."

He nodded. "Call me. I'd like to see her in a not-too-conspicuous spot."

"Leave that to me—the Intimate Bookshop."

"Is that what you call your little bordello?"

"It's on the window."

"A most appropiate name—for the occasion."

An exit speech, and I was about to rise, but he now spoke about his Memphis beauty. Her name was Rosemary. She had read *Tender Is the Night* when it first came out, and had identified with the character of the young actress, Rosemary Hoyt, who falls in love with Dr. Diver and later has a brief affair with him. Fitzgerald had smiled when she told him this, and said there might be hundreds of Rosemarys who felt the same way. She asked how many had actually met him—as she and he had, by chance.

"I told her none. It was all she needed to seize on our meeting as the hand of fate. I tried to convince her that it was a coincidence. I couldn't. I tried and couldn't. I can't explain it. The more I thought about it, the less sure I was myself. Years ago I wrote a short story with a character in it named Lois Moran. Later in Hollywood I met a young actress by that name. I was quite taken by her—her beauty and vitality. Zelda noticed it. Lois Moran was the living model for Rosemary Hoyt."

I murmured something, to show that I was listening. But I was truly engrossed.

"Rosemary gave me her key. It's in my pocket." He made a helpless gesture. "She could be another Madame Bovary with the same wild expectations. I have so little left to give, let alone passion. That takes as much out of me as pain and misery. I keep stalling, hoping for I don't know what, but I'm afraid I want her too. The way I haven't . . . since Zelda became my invalid.

"I met her sister Myra. Smaller, epicene, inhibited. She has internal trouble and seems the nervous-breakdown type. She got her brother-in-law to let Rosemary come along to Asheville and spend part of the summer with her. I think Myra resents me already—caught wind of this thing with Rosemary. She's envious of her. She could wire that fine husband in Memphis. All I need is a messy triangle."

Sober, his eyes shone with a cold blue clarity; he wasn't so much talking to me as he was following interior paths.

"I think about Zelda. Those days when I was in love with a dazzling light—I thought she was a goddess. Triumphant, proud, fearless. Going at top speed in the gayest worlds we could find. She reached and took all the things life put before her until she collapsed and could reach no more. Now she's a pathetic figure who reads her Bible. Broken, humiliated, her radiant eyes with no luster, her fiery hair a frazzled mop. Sometimes her old spirit hovers about her, sometimes it's on leave. I hold back my tears or she'll write Scottie to look after me."

There were no tears when he rose. We walked out of the hotel into the late afternoon sun. I invited him to come along to rehearsal if he was in a mood for Bach or Beethoven.

"I don't care for music. I'll drop off Hecht and pick up Joyce," he said, gesturing with the book. We shook hands. His palm was moist and shaky. "About Lottie, don't make it tomorrow. I may run over to the Flynns' for a day or two. I was to see Rosemary tonight. Feeling as I do—" He smiled unhappily, leaving another question. He started to go, hesitated. "The damnable thing is that I know this all sounds like a drowning sailor reaching for a floating oar."

6

Days passed before I arranged for Fitzgerald and Lottie to meet. He had spent most of the time in bed at the Oak Hall, a country-style hotel overlooking the main street of Tryon, where he had written what might be a salable story. Writing it had been a mild dissipation; he had kept at it when he should have been resting, but he felt he had to lift himself out of a rut. He was sending it to his agent with the usual plea for an advance on what it might bring.

We were alone in the bookshop. Freshly shaved and trimmed, dressed casually, and carrying a cane for the first time, Scott had the look of a Prince Charming. His manner was sober and calm, with no trace of dissipation or his old gloom. It was an inexplicable change, as though he and not Zelda were the schizophrenic. His attitude toward Lottie also changed; he approached his meeting with her as if she were a society woman he was taking to a ball game.

He returned with the Joyce book, saying it had been his best companion during the week. As he looked over my collection, I told him that Bill Davis had reported favorably on Highland Hospital. It was managed by Dr. Robert Carroll, a highly respected clinician who believed that toxic elements caused by deficiencies from improper diet and other factors could play a vital part in the origin of nervous diseases, and what he had learned he tried to use in their cure.

"Bill warned me against several other private hospitals and so-called retreats. He said patients were starved, tied and beaten, given countless cold showers, and their mouths taped to gag their screams—at fifty to a hundred dollars a week."

"Murderers and racketeers," he said angrily. "Are there no laws to protect the mentally ill?"

A blond, doll-like woman walked in from the Arcade, bringing with her the warm lacquer scent of the beauty shop. I took the three books she carried and went to the rental file for her card. While she chose from a shelf bearing such titles as *Stolen Rapture*, *House of Incest*, and *Forbidden Fruit*, Fitzgerald studied a frame near the desk containing letters from Faulkner, Shaw, O'Neill, Dos Passos, Anderson, Pound, Upton Sinclair, Norman Douglas, Sinclair Lewis, Mencken, and George Jean Nathan.

"I have a notion that small bookshops will become as obsolete as silent pictures because of book clubs and department-store competition," he said after my customer left with three sexy thrillers.

"I don't intend to make a career of it," I said.

"What's this magazine you edited?" he asked, turning back to the frame.

"*Contempo*. A little review published in Chapel Hill."

"A student-lit publication?"

I explained that five of us students had started it to stir up a little excitement on the country-clublike campus, but it wasn't a college publication—though enemies of the university said it was. I opened a drawer, dug out an old promotional sheet with comments by writers, some of whose letters were in the frame, and handed it to him. I told him it had lasted from 1931 through 1933, and that it had lived up to its reputation of being, as Carl Sandburg called it, "a bully, quarrelsome review." And for all its big names, we didn't pay for contributions.

"A cuckoo magazine."

"Cuckoo?" I repeated. "*The Little Review*, *Broom*, *The Double Dealer*, and *transition* were all little magazines."

"A writer has to be cuckoo to give his stuff away," he explained. "Some of them were avant-garde, some were chichi or sheer nonsense."

"They published the first stuff by Joyce and your friends Hemingway and Stein."

"Ernest had to slave away at newspaper hacking to write those first stories. I suppose I was rather snooty in the early twenties. And lucky too—got good prices after *This Side of Paradise*. I couldn't write them fast enough." He glanced at the sheet and gave me a dubious look. "Did Joyce really say, 'By way of literary immortality I read *Contempo*,' or is this a fake? His letter's not in that frame."

"Joyce wrote that letter to Milton Abernethy. The two of us ran the magazine after the other three left." He was silent, and I went on. "One went back to his father's barbershop in Newark. One is bumming in the South and writing his adventures for *The New Republic*. And the other went to Moscow with a Russian dictionary and a tractor manual under his arm to become a mechanic and said he was a tennis champ there."

Fitzgerald nodded and turned a page. "You ran a lot of poets. Jeffers, Crane, Kreymborg, Aiken, Joyce, Williams, Stevens, Pound, Aragon, Rilke, Faulkner, and Essenin, Isadora's husband. Why not Ernest and your Asheville genius?"

"They never answered us. Nor did you," I said. "You three Scribners boys shunned us. But we mailed you copies on and off just the same."

"You remembered I was still in the Big League."

"You certainly are."

"Those years I didn't exist as a serious writer. I was buried in Europe, grinding out *Post* stories to pay for Zelda's hospital bills. And trying to make headway with *Tender*." He glanced back at the sheet. "Sinclair Lewis: 'You're not on your way to success until the newspapers call you nuts, cranks and liars.' Did they?"

"Our Scottsboro number riled Southern editors as far as Montgomery." I watched his face, as that was Zelda's hometown and once the capital of the Confederacy. He let it pass. The Scottsboro case was the first nationally publicized—and ultimately successful—challenge to Southern justice as it applied to black people; it involved eight youths condemned to death for the alleged rape of two white female tramps. "Some Carolina editors blistered us with words and called for the governor to take over the magazine, claiming it was a university publication. Actually, they were gunning for Dr. Graham, the university president."

I was referring to Frank Porter Graham, the liberal, North Carolina-born head of the University of North Carolina at Chapel Hill. Dr. Graham had been bucking the power trust and the textile and tobacco barons of the state, trying to get appropriations through the legislature. He had also written a piece for *Contempo* on how the Depression affected education. The issues were still very close to me and I made what amounted to a speech on them. He appeared amused and interested.

"You sound radical. Maybe a Communist."

"If that's all it takes, count me in."

"I've been a radical as long as I can remember," he said. "A Marxist socialist since I started thinking. Wells and Shaw nudged me along those days. But I'm no joiner."

"I'm no card carrier either."

"My friend Bunny Wilson and several others have gone all the way to communism. I got pretty close, but my writer's instinct held me back. I can't afford it. It would take time from my writing. It's all I can manage to save myself and take care of Zelda and Scottie. Do you have a copy of your magazine I can see?"

"Several." I went back to the desk. "You'll see it wasn't all radical protest and social significance. We were literary, but not ivory tower. *Contempo* was a Depression baby. I took the name from a book of drawings by John Vassos, the illustrator and industrial designer. Now he's helping big business to glamorize its products."

I handed him three copies of the tabloid-sized review: the issues devoted to Faulkner, to Bernard Shaw, and the Malcolm Cowley–Gorham Munson controversy. The last concerned the founding of *Secession*, a little magazine published in France in the early twenties. The Shaw issue featured a letter he had written me about his authorized biographer, Dr. Archibald Henderson, a Chapel Hill math professor. The Faulkner number carried his first poems published in almost a decade, making it a collector's item at the time. Fitzgerald glanced at the latter and read a poem on the front page. It was about youth.

"All good writers start as poets," he said. "Rimbaud wrote that poets are both the invalids and prophets of their age."

"Faulkner's first book was poetry: *The Marble Faun*. Privately printed and a rare item today. Most of the edition was junked."

"My first sale was to *Poet Lore*. Then a story to *Smart Set*. I switched to fiction to make the big time."

"Poetry goes begging. You could've sent us a poem."

"I just had one in *The New Yorker*—the first I wrote in over ten years." He was sitting on the edge of the desk, smoking. "I must have tossed out your letter without reading it or it never got to me. Did *Contempo* pay its way?"

"We managed on milk, a hunk of cheese, and day-old bread—two loaves for the price of one."

"You and your pretty wife?"

"We were married a few months before the bank holiday. She had a dollar a day to squander on three meals—sometimes we had a dinner guest. Now with my publicity job she has almost twice as much."

"What happened to *Contempo*?"

"The same as to most little magazines. Finances and internal squabbles."

Lottie arrived at that moment and Fitzgerald jumped off the desk. He appeared charmed by her smart appearance and the vitality she radiated in the small shop. As I introduced them, she smiled and extended her hand. I noticed in her other hand a book—the copy of *The Great Gatsby* she had picked up the day before.

"Your friend's cute as a bug, but I hope all writers aren't so fussy!" Lottie seemed highly amused. I met her two days later walking her dogs near the Arcade and we sat down on a concrete slab in the shade. "The interview was in a bar. It was ducky. I ordered a cocktail. He said he was on his best behavior. I suppose it meant he was on the wagon. It turned out to be a wagon of beer. What's he like when he's on his worst?"

"Beer is his way of cutting down on hard liquor. I hope he didn't get stinko."

"He was navigating under his own steam and talking a blue streak when I poured him into a taxi. I've never heard anybody talk so sweet. Or met a man more forlorn and at loose ends. He asked for my phone number and where I lived. I told him with my two poodles, and he called me a mystery woman. I felt sorry for him."

I gathered that Lottie was reluctant to see the interview end, although Fitzgerald told her that his secretary was waiting for him at the Inn—work that he didn't think he was up to doing at that point.

"I had a date I couldn't break or I'd have gone along with him."

"He asked you?"

"Well, yes and no." Again her amusement surfaced. "I suppose the real reason I didn't go was someting he said."

When he was at Princeton, Fitzgerald told her, he hadn't chased after waitresses, chippies, dime-store clerks, or gone weekend-whoring with his chums to the big town. Lottie asked what he had done instead, but he didn't say. He told her that much as he wanted to join them, he had a horror of venereal disease; he might even have taken a chance with one of the working girls, but never with a professional like her—Lottie.

"I had to laugh. I laughed in his face. Then I wised him up plenty about amateurs. That they carry more of those unmentionables than *we* do. Ordinary girls are careless. *We* have to stay healthy and keep our looks to stay in business. And I told him I only went out with lawyers, doctors, and men who read *The Wall Street Journal*. But if he wanted a clean bill of health, I could get him one. And without batting his baby-blue eyes, you know what he said?—'I'd like to see it.' "

It was out at last. She added triumphantly, "You could've knocked me over with a feather!"

But there was more—something I wouldn't have expected from Lottie, who called her own shots. She had that very morning taken a complete physical, including a Wasserman.

"And I'm going to show him the report, too!"

I suggested that he might have asked to see it simply out of a writer's curiosity, because he hoped to do a story about a social aspect of her profession.

"He told me he tried to write about a girl like me in France, but gave up because it had to be treated with kid gloves—at least, by him. I stupidly asked how you became a writer. He said you learn by experience, like everything else, and you never become anything by wishing and praying. He said writing was a miserable and lonesome profession. I had an idea it was glamorous. I'm not so sure now." She was thoughtful. "He said I was lucky to become a member of the human race at five. He didn't until he was fifteen and it had cost him plenty. What did he mean?"

It struck me that the tables were turned: Lottie was now going after Fitzgerald's story.

I again noticed the copy of *Gatsby* and asked her if she had opened the book.

"I've read it all," she replied very seriously. "Yes, I really did!"

7

F or the next few days Lottie didn't drop by, and it wasn't until a week later that I saw Fitzgerald again. They both had a way of vanishing, Lottie to fly off to New York, Cuba, or Catalina, California, with a heavy date, Fitzgerald to see the Flynns or to go to Baltimore to visit Zelda. Sometimes he went on to New York to confer with his editor or agent. There were times when he rounded out the trip with a two- or three-day spree, alone or with friends. If it was a bang-up spree, he ended in a hospital.

It was almost midnight when I got a call from the Inn. I was in the shop finishing a book column. He was garrulous, his voice thick. I hardly understood what he said, but he made it sound urgent. He wanted me to hop a cab and go out to see him. I hesitated; taxi fare was an extravagance we couldn't afford and the bus had stopped running at that hour. He insisted he could talk to no one else.

"The worst has happened," he added. "And it's partly your fault—damn it!"

It was a dark night and the stars hung low in that high mountain country. I looked out the window as the taxi rolled into the wooded suburbs and swung around curves. The Inn was a stone-faced structure nestling in a pine grove; its elaborate entrance and tremendous fireplace gave it the air of an expensive country club. The young night clerk said Fitzgerald was talking long distance—he had been on the phone most of the evening—and that I should go up; his door was open and he was expecting me.

His back was to me when I entered the brightly lit room of knotty pine and cheerfully curtained windows. There wasn't a shadow and the paneling reflected the light like glass. Books, clothes, and papers were scattered about, ash trays piled with butts and bits of rubbish;

and there were bottles, all empty but one, which was half-full of gin, and cups, bowls, and an ornate silver coffeepot on a room-service tray precariously set near a closet door. The door was ajar; there was a large carton of empty bottles on the floor.

Fitzgerald was sitting on the edge of a flower-patterned couch, the telephone in one hand, a glass and a cigarette in the other, talking in the same hoarse voice. A dressing gown failed to cover his pale legs, which seemed short for his torso, and his stubby and unattractive feet were showing. When he saw me he fumbled for his slippers and hid his feet in them. Then he greeted me, set down the glass, and covered the mouthpiece.

"This will only take another minute."

He held out his pale white hand and went on talking. I reached for it and he gave mine a shaky grip. His eyes were strained and bloodshot, his cheeks white, and his face was unshaven. Perspiration dotted his forehead. It was a mild night yet he was wearing, underneath his gown, a woolen sweater over a pajama top.

"I have fever," he said when he hung up, wiping his forehead. "I should be in bed."

"Why aren't you?"

"I have to call these people." He came forward with his glass and put a hand on my shoulder. "Let me give you something."

"No, thank you."

"Don't need this now," he mumbled and walked unsteadily to snap off the ceiling lights. Then he picked up the gin bottle and refilled the glass, took a sip, and sat down on the couch. He pointed the drink at me as I sank into a chair. "A hell of a cure. Never fails. I see you don't get it. A drink or two more and I'll sweat out all that booze. When my fever drops I'll hop on the old wagon again. I see you still don't understand. At least you don't lecture me or ask silly questions."

He set down the glass, drew the gown closer about his shoulders, and dropped his head in his hands. He was silent; I had nothing to say. The phone rang. He picked it up, listened, then told the operator to cancel his other calls. Out of cigarettes, he asked if I had any; I shook my head and he dug among the crumpled butts, found a passable one, and lit it.

"You have no vices."

"Not obvious ones."

"Living a double life?"

"Wouldn't know how."

"I'll tell you."

It had happened with Rosemary. (According to what he told his Dollar Woman, "it had happened" a night or so before I met him, but he spoke to me as if it had just begun.) That, and other things in the preceding thirty-six hours, and he was full of them. He had made up his mind not to get involved with Rosemary and thought he had convinced her that this was the best course for her too. Knowing that she had never been unfaithful to her husband, he told her that she would be on his conscience if he were the first of several lovers.

He also warned her that it could be no more than an affair. Though Zelda was his invalid, probably for the rest of his life, he wouldn't divorce her; they had belonged to each other in the freshness of youth and all the depth that love holds. He was bound by this love and by duty to her and Scottie, to whom he had been both father and mother since Zelda's breakdown.

A love affair is like a short story, he had said—Fitzgerald was drinking when he told Rosemary this, but he assured me that he had never spoken a more sober word—it had a beginning, a middle, and an end. The beginning was easy, the middle might drag, invaded by the commonplace, but the end, instead of being decisive and knit with that element of revelatory surprise as a well-written story should be, usually was dissipated in a succession of messy and humiliating anticlimaxes. He saw the affair, pursuing his analogy for her benefit, only to the middle stage: he had a hunch that events beyond their control would terminate it before it came to its own logical and necessary conclusion.

None of this had made an impression on Rosemary. She had called him a pessimist. Fitzgerald had been so fatuous as to assure her that he was a realist, wryly commenting to me that the distinction between pessimism and realism could have no meaning to a young woman who fancied herself passionately in love. The beginning seemed within her grasp, the middle and the end were an inconceivable future.

She had come to Fitzgerald's room that night, where they had, in equal parts, talked, drunk, and made love in a limited, frustrating manner, until his moralities became a bore to her and a strain on him. He hated being lectured to and despised his own attempts to lecture someone else—at such a time. But with every drink he took, Fitzgerald became more resolved not to entangle himself. At dawn Rosemary left him and went back to her room in the Inn.

Suddenly he had felt lonely, deserted, and cheated. He cursed himself for having uttered such rubbish and letting her go. She was what he really wanted—she was young, beautiful, and wildly in love with him—what idiocy had stopped him? What man could ask for more in this tragic life where happiness was a dream belonging only to the perennially young? His reaction had run full circle in the few minutes she had gone when the phone rang. If it was Rosemary, he meant to have her back. Instead, the operator announced that a Miss Lottie was in the lobby to see him.

"I was wild," he said. He held his head in his hands. "I told the operator to send her up. Forgetting at the moment," he added, "the significance of her being a call girl—even if most of her clients did read *The Wall Street Journal*."

Lottie walked in looking as fresh as the morning, he told me, although she had spent the night with an oil baron from Oklahoma City. Fitzgerald had mentioned his insomnia and crazy hours to her; she reminded him of this by way of apologizing for her visit at such an hour. And she opened her bag and gave him her health report. (This was the first time he mentioned it, confirming Lottie's story of the test.) He looked at it, startled, and then at her with admiration for having taken such trouble for him. His request to see it had sounded smart to him; now it seemed utterly stupid.

Holding the drink he gave her, Lottie sat back on the couch with an air of ease and freedom, crossing her beautiful long legs. It was dim in his mind what further conversation took place. There were no strings attached to Lottie. Already given over to desire, he needed no encouragement. In a few minutes the delightful Lottie stood like a vision before him. It was only later that he remembered with distaste that an oil millionaire had shortly preceded him.

At any rate, he hoped that this incident would shake his senses back to normal. It wasn't to be. On the contrary, it served to increase his feeling for the Memphis beauty. The casual experience with Lottie only provoked his deeper hunger: his need for someone who loved him. Love, even temporary and insubstantial, had become a necessity to him out of his own despair and his sense of loss over Zelda. The night before, then, there was the beginning of his love affair with Rosemary.

"I don't blame you for Lottie," he said finally. "She's okay—it's me. Women and liquor have always gotten me into trouble. But this means I'm losing control. Letting myself go downhill with a whore and then getting involved in an affair that's bound for disaster—when I've hit bottom and there's scarcely one more emotion in me. Yes, I blame myself. I've always been the victim of my weaknesses. And my greatest one now is a craving for excitement. Christ, how it stimulates me! I need it to pull myself together. To fight off this depression and get back on top. It gives me the illusion I'm still young."

How he had made the turnabout, I don't know. It was a night of self-recrimination, of concern for morality that verged on the sentimental, of sentiment that touched on the maudlin, and the last of any booze in the room. It was past dawn; I opened the curtains and the sky was bright with sunshine.

At that early hour Fitzgerald seemed more alive than I did, more youthful and eager for whatever the new day might bring. The gown hung loosely about his shoulders, the perspiration had vanished from his forehead. It seemed that his old cure must have worked. At the door he held my hand and apologized for going on about himself without having asked about my concerns.

But now he had work to do, he said calmly. He had hit on a story idea. No, it had nothing to do with Lottie and her gamy profession. If the story came off, he was sure some of his kind friends—those who predicted an early alcoholic grave for him—would notice that he was still among the living and writing. And he would start on it as soon as he got cigarettes and coffee.

8

Fitzgerald's writing mood carried him through the new story and into another that seemed to take off from it. An earlier story—the one he had written in Tryon—and been rejected by *The Saturday Evening Post* and was now being considered by a magazine paying a fraction of the price he usually commanded. Yet except for his mounting debts, everything seemed to be going his way for the moment.

He had told me two things were helpful in his writing: a drink to sharpen his mind and senses, and the stimulation of love-making to put his creative imagination into high gear. (Love-making for this purpose, instead of for the sheer pleasure of it, may have caused part of his sexual troubles, as Lottie was to tell me later.) These had become a need that he tried to satisfy before putting pencil to paper.

"Maybe you think I'm oversexed. I am and was long before I knew it. But I'm not the only artist who works that way. There's Picasso. I hear he needs his wine, his woman, and friends to give him the drive to tackle one of his compositions."

Fitzgerald decided to accept Rosemary as a gift from the gods, regardless of the consequences, for the sake of his writing. His work was the only thing he now enjoyed, so he said; idleness put him in a scrappy and depressed mood. As for drinking in this situation, it served to block his Puritan conscience. This may sound quaint today, but the sexual strictures of that heritage weighed heavily on earlier generations. In Scott there was a specifically Catholic cast to that conscience; he even told me he had considered the priesthood. His sensuality had frightened him since his early teens and he tried to ignore or curb it, imbued as he was with the concept of the flesh as sinful and evil.

But there were rewards beyond the sexual in his relations with

Rosemary. She seemed to give him, he said, a return of his youth, with a promise of a renewed life. It was something he needed but thought he had lost with Zelda and would never recapture. And though grateful for her gift, there were moments when he saw Rosemary for what she was: an ordinary young woman of the leisure class, with the insensitivity peculiar to her kind, limited in mental scope and having no dazzling inner light or sense of wonder, only the possessive urgency of her passion.

Fitzgerald spoke of being oversexed and of his relations with Rosemary after perusing André Tridon's *Psychoanalysis*, an early popular Freudian study. We left the shop and went to a restaurant in Pack Square where he often drank more than he ate. It was midafternoon; he appeared sober though he had consumed several beers and ales. I left him there and put in an appearance at the symphony office. That night I jotted down his comments on the flyleaf of the Tridon book.

When I saw him again I was on my way to rehearsal. He decided to go with me, even if he didn't care for music and knew nothing about it. He wanted to meet my boss and publicity instructor, Lamar Stringfield, conductor of the North Carolina Symphony and composer of *From the Southern Mountains*, for which he had been awarded a Pulitzer Prize. The work was based on tunes of the Carolina mountain folk; its most popular section was the finale, "Cripple Creek," a rollicking jig, which Lamar used as an encore at all his concerts.

I hesitated to take Fitzgerald along, fearing that my amiable mentor might invite him to sample his choice Carolina corn or rye, which he got from its law-defying makers. Lamar liked to say that the mist over the Blue Ridge Mountains was nothing more than blue smoke rising from moonshiners' stills. That day Fitzgerald was on the wagon; if they started tippling and he fell off it, I would be to blame. He noticed my reluctance.

"I'm a solitary toper," he assured me.

I changed the subject and began telling him that Lamar had an instinct for publicity—at least for himself—and his suggestions rarely missed. I also mentioned that Lamar was a baseball fan. This pleased Scott. He was one himself, although his favorite sport was football. Inadvertently I got back on the subject of drinking by saying that Lamar had fallen off the podium twice that season before audiences of hundreds.

"I've done about everything but that—unless my memory fails me," he said. "You make Lamar sound worth meeting."

Fitzgerald asked how I had become involved with another drinking man. It was because the orchestra was to summer in Asheville, I said, and I wanted to come there because of Wolfe. That April I had interviewed Stringfield in Durham for the United Press. When I went to see him in his hotel suite, he was scoring a new work, *Moods of a Moonshiner*, at a drawing board while the radio churned out loud hillbilly music. He looked up at me from under his green eyeshade and said, "This is how a genius works."

"Lamar was dead serious when he said this," I told Fitzgerald. "He liked my story and asked me to be his press agent. I didn't know what that meant then. That didn't stop Lamar. He said he'd teach me."

"Your switch from journalism to ballyhoo must have been tough," he said.

"Yes." Then I went on to tell him that my present assignment was to publicize a children's concert. The price of admission was a penny postcard. As a picture stunt I thought of a boy and girl presenting either the mayor or a music-club official with a blowup of the card as an admission ticket to the concert. But Lamar had a better idea: a moppet with him and Tina, his black scotty. He said he preferred being photographed with them to posing beside politicians or musical dowagers.

"Kids and animals are page-one pets," he said. And as I told this to Fitzgerald, I added, "Lamar's a publicity hound, but he knows his stuff."

America had amused itself not long before with stories and pictures of flagpole sitters and marathon dancers. That carnival was over, and newspapers were now featuring panaceas to beat the Depression: NRA, WPA, FDR's fireside chats, Upton Sinclair's barter cooperatives, and Huey Long's Share the Wealth scheme. Everybody was talking about such books as *Life Begins at Forty*, *Wake Up and Live*, and *How to Make Friends and Influence People*. But children and animals always made news, and Lamar wasn't above using them to promote himself along with symphonic music.

In time I originated a story, I told Fitzgerald. I thought it out as I watched his dog Tina react to the instruments tuning up at rehearsal. The violins made her growl, trumpets perked up her ears, and her master's flute started her rolling on her back for play. When the story appeared as a United Press item, he avoided me. I had made the unpardonable mistake of putting her name—not his—in the first paragraph. Those days I was ignorant about billing, chronic fever of the entertainment world.

"Like that dog I want to howl when I hear certain notes."

"You had a dog story in *Esquire* recently, 'Shaggy's Morning.' "

"It was god-awful." Then he fell silent for a moment. "I knew a writer with your composer's special talent," he said at last. "He harassed his editor and publisher with ideas and gimmicks to promote his novels. He wrote his own advertising copy, jacket blurbs, and publicity notes, selected quotes from critics and friends, raised bloody murder over colors and photographs of himself, and wasted time dreaming up tie-ins. He was stung by the same ballyhoo bug to exploit himself as your composer."

"I hope he got better results."

"It probably helped to make him the only best-seller who didn't sell any more." He studied me as though I should recognize the writer he referred to. "There was a cheap side to his talent. Sometimes it got the better of him. He had the gall to advertise his first novel in the last chapter of his second—"

"That was you."

I suddenly remembered the successful young novelist in *The Beautiful and Damned* who said that everywhere he went some silly girl would ask him if he had read *This Side of Paradise*.

"I once had your composer's egotism of a maniac. I now see it an expression of youthful exuberance. Of course, I would have done better if I could have advertised my second in my first. The first was my biggest seller, and with hardly any advertising from Scribners. I was sore at the time and crabbed like hell because a mediocre novel like Floyd Dell's *Moon Calf* was being touted by its publisher with big ads. Nevertheless I found my public of flappers and college youths, but they have dwindled through the years from a hundred thousand to less than five thousand for *Taps*. I once was a kind of oracle to them."

Fitzgerald said that he wrote the bulk of his first two novels in St. Paul, and though hailed by the local press as the city's first major author, he still resented Minnesota's giving its main attention to Sinclair Lewis. Both he and Lewis had been concerned with the rags-to-riches American success story, he said; Lewis satirized the new wealthy middle class and added a word to the dictionary: babbitt, while he himself tended to dig into the lonely and tragic void behind the pretentious façade.

"My first novel had wide appeal. It pleased young and old, conservatives, liberals, rebels, even the radical press. In the closing chapter my hero becomes a spokesman for socialism as a way that should be tried to get the most out of the best men in finance and the professions. The second book didn't have as many friends. It was self-conscious and smart. My aim was to attack the middle class like Flaubert with Menckenian wit and savagery: its money values, beliefs, religion—I almost lost a great friend because of my attack on religion."

He then asked if I had stopped saying my beads for the salvation of my soul in a Roman Catholic heaven as he, Joyce, Dreiser, and other writers had done. I replied that I had been on the way out of the church when some hypocrites and a nudge from Mencken had made it impossible for me ever to fall on my knees again. He asked whether I had replaced religion with anything. I answered that I had simply got rid of excess baggage.

"You're luckier than I. Or we potato-famine Irish take things a lot harder than you volatile and violent Latins. After I dropped away from the church, I kept saying I wanted to become a priest. Probably it was because I fancied myself the wickedest youth in the world, and I must say I enjoyed the idea of renunciation, too. It happened twice while I was at Princeton—when my first love refused me, and later while visiting my friend John Bishop, who introduced me to the pleasures of English poetry. And again later, in a Southern army camp when I got word that Monsignor Fay, the best friend of my youth—the Monsignor Darcy of *Paradise*—died in the flu epidemic.

"Probably I was kidding myself or play-acting, out of my sense of loss and shock. I got over the idea of wanting to become a priest and the gap with religion widened. Some of my friends have said that when I stopped going to Mass I started drinking. Even if that were true, it would be only part true. About that time I was digging into Marxism, socialism and communism. I have since discovered that *that* can be a religion too. At least it is for some of my friends who are now hot on the subject. You said you weren't a card-carrying radical. But I wonder if you aren't the kind of renegade who has replaced the Apostle's Creed with the Communist Manifesto."

It was too late to answer him. We had arrived at the side entrance of the high-school building, set off by tall pines and magnolias. I opened the heavy door and led him into the empty auditorium. The orchestra was onstage; the men had their sleeves rolled up and Lamar was conducting from a raised platform, his white shirttails out and swinging with his baton. We took a seat at the back and watched his gyrations instead of listening to the music.

"Vitality to match his egotism," was Fitzgerald's sole comment.

In a few minutes Lamar slammed his stick and gave the men a break. He hopped off the stage and came toward us with a cordial smile forming under his dark mustache. His dark hair and eyes could have placed him as a Latin, though his family was English and one of the first in Carolina.

"It's an honor to have you, Mr. Fitzgerald," he said when I introduced them. "I'm giving this concert at Grove Park Inn Friday. I hope you and your friends will be my guests."

"Thank you."

"Mozart opens the program," he said, gesturing with a long cigarette holder. "I'm featuring the Beethoven First and Stravinsky's *Firebird*. I don't know your musical taste but I believe there's something for everybody in this concert."

"Call me a lowbrow," Fitzgerald said. "Kern, Herbert, Romberg, Friml, Youmans, Porter, Gershwin, Rodgers and Hart."

"Of course, Mr. Fitzgerald!" Lamar said, with a smile of recognition. "Fox trots, waltzes, and jazz. You're the father of the Jazz Age!"

He expected Fitzgerald to acknowledge it but there was a short silence.

"I want you to know, Mr. Fitzgerald, that serious composers are with it," he went on. "Jazz has invaded the concert halls and is holding its own. Milhaud, Ravel, Stravinsky, and Martinu have composed jazz works. I'd like to play a *Show Boat* medley to show you that your taste isn't as lowbrow as you think."

"That's nice of you."

"I've been one of your most devoted readers in *The Saturday Evening Post*. For a while I wondered if you weren't its number-one pet or you owned a piece of it." He laughed and winked at me as if to show me how he sold himself. But I was pleased to see he wasn't doing too well with Fitzgerald. "Perhaps we can have a drink. None of those dainty cocktails, but straight from a jug of mountain dew."

"Most kind of you. I'm on the wagon."

"Too bad—this stuff's worth falling off for. But I wouldn't come between you and your noble resolutions."

Lamar drew me aside for a whispered conference about our visitor. I was eager to leave at that point, divided as I was between loyalty to my friend and the somewhat elastic duties of my job. Then I led Fitzgerald out of the building.

"Stick around," Fitzgerald said dryly. "He'll make a press agent out of you yet."

"He just asked me to send out a release on your meeting and play up the jazz angle. I stalled him by saying it should wait until you came to the concert."

"I'll go if you want me to."

"No, thanks. I won't give him the chance to expect first billing over you, even if he has won a Pulitzer Prize."

"Maybe you'd better tell him I once turned down the Literary Guild."

That summer Fitzgerald showed no further interest in Lamar and his ideas to ballyhoo himself.

—————————9

"It is easy to be loved, so hard to love," Fitzgerald said at the time. "I have the awful feeling I'm using Rosemary and giving her little. She wants so much to love me, to do everything she can to pull me out of the dumps. A big order, more than she can manage, with all her youth and money. She offered me a signed blank check to settle my debts. About forty thousand. And a monthly allowance for Zelda and Scottie, so I wouldn't have to worry about them."

It was the first time such an offer had come his way, and from a beautiful young woman. Much as he frowned on the idea of being a gigolo, he knew she didn't mean it that way. It was a spontaneous gesture, like buying him denicotinized cigarettes. He had told her about his siege of tuberculosis; she thought these would hurt him less if he couldn't give up the habit.

Rosemary insisted that she loved him more than she had loved her husband. And that she didn't mind if Fitzgerald never said he loved her. But the situation was becoming a bit difficult for him: he found it impossible to shut her out. He was forced to stop her numerous phone calls. She responded by writing love notes and slipping them under his door or sending them, by a bellboy, with a knitted tie, a carton of cigarettes, or a box of sweets. Knowing he was fond of candy, she hoped he would reach for it instead of taking another drink.

On nights when he didn't see her, he told Rosemary that he was busy on a story or with his secretary. She would be hurt because he was shutting her out, and left with the feeling that it was her fault. He told her that it was his, not hers—his inability to love her or another woman. Yet Fitzgerald knew he was too much for her, too extreme and difficult a person, and far out of her ken. He thoughtlessly mentioned this to her one night. She fell asleep in his arms, and he let himself go and bawled with her.

Fitzgerald now blamed himself rather than Rosemary's pursuit of him for starting the affair. It was the nature of his charm, he said; it served him well. He won hearts with this charm: a combination of his fame, his ability to make each one feel she was his only woman, his conversation sprinkled with praise of their beauty and analysis of their vagrant emotions, and his tender romantic appeal, which disguised a strong sexuality.

In the midst of the affair he thought constantly of Zelda's tragedy, her loss of self, spirit, and her radiant being. Zelda's breakdown had brought a change that went beyond time's relentless role of sapping her vitality and youth. He had disliked the thought of getting old and had regretted not dying like Keats at the peak of his talent and years. Now he lamented the fact that in September he would be thirty-nine.

Youth meant beauty and vitality to him, he said, and to lose it was life's greatest sorrow. The acceptance of the change was a sign of maturity, his friends had told him; some of them believed that he was a Peter Pan who might never grow up. He was conscious of not growing up in the accepted way—to forget one's dreams and shut out the sense of wonder and possibility inherent in the young.

Time had a way of freeing emotions, he also said, so we wouldn't be haunted forever by our mistakes and tragedies. As our capacity to feel loss diminished, memories grew dimmer, feelings less intense and more bearable. He spoke of this when mentioning Zelda's vanished self. It now affected him more poignantly in memory than when he was with her; he felt more pity than love for her and his grief was no longer all-encompassing. With this realization a new sadness crept over him: the thought that, because of the steady erosion of his ability to feel this loss, he didn't possess his old emotional intensity and depth.

Through the years I have been asked why Fitzgerald revealed so much to me about Zelda's tragedy, his affairs with women, and his innermost feelings. I believe it could have been his loneliness and feeling of being isolated in the mountain resort, together with my bookshop, which kept him in touch with the literary world, my being a struggling young writer whom he wanted to help, and my having the quality that he said most attracted him—vitality.

Most of all, I believe, it was Fitzgerald himself and what his biographers call his "talent for intimacy." This gift is responsible for a warmth that glows in his best writing. He reached out to people and swept into his orbit those who attracted him. It was an impulsive gesture, almost deliberate at times and not too discriminating, yet one felt it was always sincere. He revealed himself suddenly and flattered one with a show of genuine concern that gave rise to friendship and trust. As I have said, that summer Fitzgerald needed friends to listen to him and to reassure him of his worth, and I was available whenever he asked to see me.

When he mentioned his diminishing grief over Zelda and the steady erosion of his ability to feel loss, he said that it was no new sensation to him. He had described it at length in the deterioration of Gloria and Anthony in *The Beautiful and Damned.* He believed it was a kind of hunch and it had caught up with him, as if he had seen a decade earlier their present predicament and his inability to feel because he no longer possessed his old emotional intensity. He now lamented this loss and, at times, heaped abuse upon himself for not having heeded the warning.

It wasn't until ten years ago that I pieced together the events of the Rosemary affair to my satisfaction. Before reading Laura Hearne's diary, I had a collection of bits and scenes that Fitzgerald had reported, and Lottie had filled me in with information she had picked up from him. What he told me wasn't always chronological; rather it was what was uppermost in his mind at the moment, and I never took the liberty of asking him to explain the missing or confusing events. There is no need to retell in this memoir the full melodrama of that summer's love, tears, and near-tragedy. Most of the details are set down in his Dollar Woman's day-by-day account.

There are loopholes and inconsistencies in the story. Fitzgerald was either tired of the affair or was too concerned about its consequences, or at times was so steeped in beer or booze that he didn't know the score; or, being the artist that he was, he simply chose to tell the incidents that were interesting to him. There is still another aspect to it all: what his writer's instinct and imagination did to the events in verbalizing them. In a later chapter there is more about this, and in his own words.

Fitzgerald never referred to Rosemary's husband or sister by name; I call him Ogden and her Myra. One of the events he told me out of chronology—it happened between Ogden's two visits to Asheville—concerned Rosemary's sister. Until Fitzgerald's appearance at the Inn, Rosemary had been attentive to Myra because of her illness. This was despite her knowledge that Myra had always hated her; but the moment Rosemary fell in love with him she had little time for her ailing sister.

The affair was a secret to Myra until she found them lunching in a cosy corner of the Inn dining room; that was after the romance had become common gossip among the hotel staff and some of the guests. Myra disliked Fitzgerald on sight and resented what he was doing to her sister. She warned Rosemary that she was endangering her health with excessive drinking and late hours, and wrecking her marriage with a fine husband by her disgraceful conduct. And she blamed Fitzgerald for having ruined her pleasant situation in the quiet mountain resort.

At first he thought she was selfish and demanding, and this irritated him so that he ignored her. Then he considered her illness and, knowing what he did about mental cases, he decided to be more understanding and make an ally of her. He met with the hostility he had expected; then quietly, persuasively, he encouraged her to talk about herself and suggested that she try a psychiatrist in Baltimore or New York. He made an effort to see the sisters together and on those occasions the spotlight was on Myra.

But whenever Fitzgerald tried too hard to resolve a delicate situation, it usually ended in disaster, or so I recall his telling me at the time. This one with Myra was no exception. Sitting in her room alone with her, he placed his arm about her shoulder in a gesture of friendly affection. She took it as a sexual advance, rose from the couch, and bolted from the room. He was so astounded by her act that he promptly got drunk.

That night Lottie encountered Fitzgerald in the Inn lobby, and from her I learned that he invited her for a drink and told her about Rosemary's outraged sister. It was as though they were old friends, she said; and Lottie was highly amused by the story; in fact, she found it hilarious. She had already noticed him with the two sisters in the dining room. Once she almost stopped by their table to say hello, but after studying the pair she passed up the chance.

When I asked her why, Lottie said the younger-looking one seemed shy and pleasant, the other priggish and had the face of a snob. Myra struck Lottie as the kind of wealthy woman whose husband would be her best and most generous client. She could see that Myra had been brought up to fear and hate sex; to such women sex was—to use a phrase that Lottie had picked up—"a matter of dignified acquiescence instead of passionate cooperation." And she was surprised to notice that Fitzgerald was more attentive to Myra than to the other sister, who was prettier and would offer no resistance to his advances.

"Some men don't know about women and make it tough for themselves. Your friend's one of them." Lottie sounded too sure of herself for me to say that Fitzgerald was involved with Rosemary; she would find out, if she were to see more of him. "But he doesn't surprise me any more. Not after reading his book. I don't know if I told you, but we were together early one morning."

"Well," I said, showing no surprise.

"He was nervous and I thought maybe that was why he was so quick about it. I asked him if that was his usual way and he said, yes, so I didn't take it personally, like he wanted to get it over with. Of course, I've known all kinds, but I expected a man who writes about love to know better. So I told him, if I saw him again, I'd give him a few tips, if he was interested. He seemed to be, so he asked me for my phone number. I gave him the Canine Château."

It wasn't until the next day that Fitzgerald heard from Rosemary, who was angry with him for giving her sister such a shock. When he explained to her, she understood about her sister, yet she told him what Myra had said to her about him: "He's not content to ruin your life. He wants to ruin mine too."

————————10

The day before Ogden's arrival in Asheville, Fitzgerald came out of the affair as he might on sobering up after a long drunk. He told Rosemary he had had enough of her; he ignored her tears and was deaf to her reproaches. Though he felt a touch of guilt, his conscience was largely clear; he had warned her that the affair could be no more than an interlude. To prolong it was to waste time and energy he needed for his writing.

It turned out that he didn't give her up for long.

Though he enjoyed the attention of women, he was at the moment fed up with their company and the emotional upheavals that went with it. Rosemary wanted to leave her husband and start a new life with him. Her sister was a neurotic who hated them both and was on the verge of a breakdown. Nora Flynn, for all her loving concern, kept after him to try Christian Science for his drinking. Only his Dollar Woman was considerate enough to let him alone.

It was one of the times when he preferred his "own lousy company" or that of another man, as I recall him saying when he dropped in for a book. His mood wasn't talkative but subdued and somewhat depressed; he was nervous and, although liquor was on his breath, he was sober and calm. He stepped over to my collection and reached for *Mosquitoes*, saying he wanted to compare Faulkner's treatment of his friend Sherwood Anderson to Hemingway's cruel satire in *The Torrents of Spring*. Faulkner had inscribed the flyleaf in his tiny hand.

"This his handwriting?" he asked. "It's minute and stunted."

"A sharp contrast to your quick, expansive, and formless—"

"Scrawl," he interjected.

"Yes," I said with a smile. "It certainly shows the extreme differences in your styles, characters, and temperaments." He appeared interested in the remark, and I went on. "The inscription is that Joyce poem you like. He wrote it down with the words, 'To Tony who can't remember.' His own memory slipped three times. For Joyce's *loveward*, he has 'moonward'; for *loveblown*, 'lovelorn'; and for the phrase *prairie grasses sighing*, 'wind in the grass sighing.'"

"Improving on Joyce?"

"He'd had a spot too many of Carolina corn that night or his handwriting would have been jewel-like. He laughed at critics who said he was influenced by Joyce's stream of consciousness or Dostoevski's morbidity, and boasted in his wry way of not having read either."

"Most critics are jackasses," he said. "That goes for college professors who pick over the bones of writers and come up with startling discoveries about trifles. I've heard Faulkner consumes a lot of booze. Do you know if it's true?"

"He tipples while working, but holds it with dignity."

"A talent I don't have."

It seemed he wanted to know about Faulkner's drinking habits so he wouldn't feel too bad about his own. If he himself had to drink, probably Faulkner's image was a good one.

"At least he gets good booze. There's a funny Hollywood story about him, but I never heard he engaged in any public shenanigans like me or Ernest."

"When did you meet Faulkner?"

"During the hullabaloo over *Sanctuary*."

Another prodding from Fitzgerald and I told him about the slight, soft-spoken, graying Southern gentleman who paid us a week's visit at Chapel Hill. Bill arrived with Milt Abernethy, who had been in New York; Milt confided that Hal had gotten him to take Bill South for fear that another publisher might take the writer away from him. Bill brought along a light valise and a zipper bag containing the almost completed manuscript of *Light in August*. He had been in New York autographing a limited edition of *Idyll in the Desert*, and seemed unmoved by the success of *Sanctuary*.

Faulkner stayed with us at the Tankersley Building in Shirley Carter's room; Shirley was one of our editors and a poet friend of Sherwood Anderson. He had decorated the room with a Doré-like nightmare in charcoal during a mad weekend's inspiration while we cheered him on; he had crisscrossed the walls with life-sized drawings of muscular figures in heroic combat. Bill was unaware of the pictorial tumult around him. He slept and rested, drank fruit jars of moonshine we got from a Negro bootlegger, and talked about his two hobbies, hunting and flying.

After the first couple of days Faulkner asked us where he was, saying he had to see Hal again before going back to Oxford. Whenever we asked him whether he cared for a "jolly spot," his word for a drink, he would nod his trim head and cheerfully drawl, "I don't mind if I do."

We had kept him incommunicado at his request. When he sobered up a bit, he smoothed his ragged thin mustache and announced, "I want out." A barber was called in to shave him and shape his mustache; we shined his shoes and took his suit to have it pressed. Bill emerged like a little dandy. We took snapshots of him, one with the hint of a smile, for our rogues' gallery of writers who had visited us.

While I was telling this to Fitzgerald, he stroked his almost invisible little blond mustache.

It was Halloween when Bill emerged, and he asked about local festivities. We said there were none and went on a witch's ride to Durham seeking excitement. The most we could find was a gang of masked young people; we followed them up an alley to a noisy party. We looked in, decided it wasn't for us, and went to the Carolina Theater. Katharine Hepburn—Scott's favorite actress—was starring in a new comedy. Bill scanned the poster and said in his usual quiet way, "Let's go in." Inside an usher led us down to the front of the dark auditorium with images flashing on the screen. "Let's go," Bill said about fifteen minutes later. "Too much talk. I want to talk."

We started back for Chapel Hill. The village was dark and tranquil. A lone neon flickered over a café; it was Harry's and we went there for sandwiches and beer. Afterward we met Phillips Russell, the playwright Paul Green's brother-in-law, who apologized to Faulkner because the university library couldn't afford any of his books and then invited him to address his writing class. Bill accepted his apology and invitation.

"Form? Form? What form?" Faulkner repeated in that class the next day when asked about his writing, the way he developed his characters, themes, and situations. "You write and you write. If it's good, it has form. If it's not, there is no such thing. All the king's horses can't make it happen."

That was the story much as I told it to Fitzgerald.

"Form is literary discipline," he said, coming out of his silence. "It may come naturally to Faulkner, but it doesn't mean he can always be sure of achieving it that way. It takes planning and clear thinking, a sense of restraint, and a wise selection of material. This is something Wolfe's work lacks and Flaubert has. Conrad too. Form is what makes the artist and his work a piece of art."

Fitzgerald signaled for me to go on. I told him that while Bill slept those first days, Milt Abernethy and I had peeked in the bag which contained the manuscript of *Light in August*. The zipper was broken and the pages were curled up in the bag, loose and unprotected. Bill had smiled when we told him we couldn't decipher his minute handwriting; he said only Louise Bonino, Harrison Smith's secretary, could read it, and she typed his manuscripts for the printer. We boldly asked if he would give us a fragment of it for *Contempo*.

"I'll have to ask Hal." He saw our disappointed faces and added, "I have stacks of poems and stories yellowing in my files back home. I'll send you some when I get back."

I was to spend that Christmas with my family in Louisiana, so Bill invited me to visit him on the way and pick up the material. When the time came, I spent a week between the Oxford hotel in the courthouse square and Faulkner's recently purchased old mansion. He had had an eye on the rundown property for years, and was now having it put in shape. His workroom was a shambles; there were gaps in the walls and flooring, the wainscoting was a sorry sight, and chunks of plaster lay in piles near his writing table, his filing cabinet, and his hunting gear.

"I couldn't give the stuff away when I wrote it," Bill said as I looked over typed copies of stories and poems which were rust-stained with old paper clips. "Now I get wires asking for them. I read them over to see if they're still good, have them typed over again, and send them off. I sometimes get a thousand for a story. They aren't that good but I take the money—to fix up this place. A piece of writing, like any work of art, has its own value aside from the market."

Fitzgerald was growing restless, but he kept me talking about Faulkner. He said it was like watching a movie; he sometimes went to one to keep from drinking. I told him that Bill wrote at a long, wide table with a jar of moonshine and a jug of fresh well water at his side. He drank while working, pouring water and liquor into a tall glass that stood near his right hand. He wrote on yellow, legal-sized sheets, keeping to the right-hand two-thirds of the paper, his pen moving up and down, evenly and without a pause, while he completely absorbed himself in his imagined world.

On his worktable was a small portable phonograph which he used to wind by hand to play Paul Whiteman's recording of *Rhapsody in Blue*. Bill said that listening to the George Gershwin music had heightened the mood he wished to maintain in *Sanctuary;* it had helped set the jazzlike tone and rhythmic suspense of his Gothic tale. He confided that he had written the book in chronological order, but after finishing it he had shifted chapters in order to create mystery and tension and thus hold his baffled readers. Popeye's story, originally at the beginning, was placed at the end. It was a trick, he admitted; he tried it to help make the book sell after his five earlier failures.

"I did something of the sort with *Gatsby*," Fitzgerald said. "I didn't shift chapters, but took the first one out entirely. It was Gatsby's background. I published it as a short story two years before *Gatsby*. Cutting it from the book served in the same way to create mystery, tension, and suspense. I believe that helped to make *Gatsby* a success."

Faulkner was living alone in the mansion at the time of my visit, except for an old Negro couple who took care of the place and his needs. He and I dined in a large empty room; man and wife served us, standing stiffly in white at our side like waiters in a small Southern hotel. I made a point of telling Fitzgerald that the trio seemed bound together by the paternalism of the old plantation system; the couple were devoted to Faulkner—his loyal "darkies," he their beloved master.

Fitzgerald had frowned on my attitude toward Negroes; this remark about the old paternalism brought a sharp rebuke from him. He had objected to my novel with a Negro hero, ignored my resistance to his bias against the hotel doorman talking to Lottie, and barely commented on *Contempo*'s forthright defense of the Scottsboro boys sentenced to death. He was sensitive to my intent in the Faulkner story and apparently felt the need to challenge me directly.

"Coming from Louisiana, you must know Negroes are happier in the South than in the North," he said. "They're appreciated as individuals, although I must admit they're considered inferior. The North pays lip service to the principle of racial equality and scorns Negroes as individuals. At times you seem to be following the Communist line. I had enough of that in Baltimore. And of Bunny Wilson, who signed that manifesto supporting Foster and *Ford*, the black man, in the election three years ago." He suddenly dropped the subject and returned with the greatest interest to Faulkner. "But you haven't told me about Faulkner's wife. Did you meet her?"

"Yes," I said.

Estelle had been Bill's dream girl, unavailable when he was a struggling young writer, and she then married and went to China with her husband. Bill was a nobody, doing odd jobs of house-painting, clerking in a New York bookstore, and running the campus post office at the University of Mississippi in Oxford. It was rumored that Bill read the mail, not out of personal curiosity but to get material for his tales. When Estelle's marriage broke up in the Orient, she returned to Oxford, bringing back a small family. Bill had gained a reputation by then, and the slight, fluttery woman who was something of a belle married him.

One night as we sat by the fireplace in the old house, Estelle, who was staying with her mother during the alterations, joined us. She was dressed for a party and had evidently had a few drinks, for she nagged Bill because he wouldn't learn to dance. "I love to dance," she kept saying. "Bill likes to tell stories." She rose and waltzed about the darkened room like an enchanted belle at a ball. Remembering stories of Zelda's rising and dancing to her own music in empty ballrooms, I watched Fitzgerald at that point. He shut his eyes and put a hand to his face.

I told him that Bill and Estelle seemed to pay little attention to each other, as though they were living in different worlds. After a while, on this evening, she sank into the chair facing us. Bill told a story and quietly smoked his pipe; he appeared to be speaking to me instead of to both of us. Her eyes were on the dancing flames and her thoughts were far from what he was saying. Before he had finished she announced that Bill had received a wire from Hollywood, asking him to name his own terms. She picked at him because he didn't care to go. He eventually went because he needed the money.

"I later learned we were both in Hollywood at the same time, but we didn't know it," Fitzgerald said. "The story goes that he was working on his own stuff."

One afternoon Bill walked me around the countryside and showed me some of Yoknapatawpha County, of which he was "sole owner and proprietor." Starting at the courthouse, he said, "Temple Drake testified there. . . . Christmas did his killing in that old house. . . . The bank Byron Snopes robbed. . . . Benbow's place. . . . Up that road near the river Wash Jones killed Sutpen. . . . The bridge that washed away and made it hard for Anse and his sons to cross with Addie's body. . . . The barn where Popeye raped Temple with a corncob. . . ."

A few weeks after I had returned to Chapel Hill, and our all-Faulkner issue was a literary scoop for having published his first verse in eight years, Faulkner wired us about a missing page from the *Light in August* manuscript. He needed it badly because he couldn't reconstruct the passage. We didn't have it, and I never learned whether he found it. But knowing how Bill wrote, with no detailed plan but from direct spontaneous invention, the novel may have been published without that page—its absence thus adding another wrinkle to mystify readers and critics.

What seemed to strike Fitzgerald most about Faulkner were the parallels in their lives. That summer he seemed to be looking for such parallels with others. Neither novelist was a man of action, but they both drank heavily in their personal and professional pursuits, were influenced by the Symbolist poets and the Southern romantic tradition of gentility; they were moralists in their outlook and sentiments; and they had married Southern belles who had rejected them until they showed signs of success.

Zelda and Estelle were products of the upper-class mores of adjoining states, Alabama and Mississippi; a sensible belle was expected to marry the man best equipped to maintain her in style and ladylike comfort. Fitzgerald remarked sadly that this emphasis on money in our culture had profoundly influenced his outlook on life and colored much of his writing.

And he added that, of the two men, he had been the more fortunate—at the beginning. He had won the sought-after girl in the flush of his youth, while Faulkner had to wait a decade for his to come back to him.

11

Late one morning Fitzgerald called me, and arranged to meet at the George Vanderbilt coffee shop. He was highly agitated; his eyes were bloodshot, his hands white, shaky, and perspiring, and there was mint on his breath. After mentioning Rosemary in a gruff whisper, he complained of hollowness in the pit of his stomach. He said it usually came from worry, fear, and insomnia, but he was sure it was now caused by too much black coffee. I watched him gulp down two cups as if he were bent on punishing himself for having an affair with her.

That morning he was worried that her husband might find out about it. In order to keep him at a safe distance, Rosemary had arranged for him to stay at Highlands, some miles away, a mountain resort. She gave as her excuse Myra's internal troubles and that she had to take care of her. But instead of spending time with her sister, Rosemary continued seeing Fitzgerald, who both wanted her and was trying to avoid her. Ogden phoned from time to time to speak with her or to invite her to lunch; there were times when Rosemary wasn't at the hotel and Myra lied to protect her. It was no wonder Fitzgerald saw himself faced with the messy triangle he had anticipated—if he didn't make a move to prevent it.

Fitzgerald confided that he was overwhelmed by another kind of fear—"anxiety" we would call it today. Anxiety not so much over Rosemary's husband and the kind of satisfaction that he might want if he learned about the affair, but one stirred up by the bitter memory of once having been in such a situation—that of the cuckolded husband. The memory was related to the most distressing aspect of his life with Zelda. Though he was now in the favored role of the lover, he felt somewhat guilty and in too shaky and confused a state to enjoy it.

He couldn't stay at the Inn, Fitzgerald said. He had to find a place or leave Asheville while her husband was there. If he went to another hotel, he could easily be traced, unless he registered under an assumed name. This was something he had done before; he wouldn't try it now for fear of being recognized (though he was to do so later that summer). He asked me to recommend a place in town until he decided whether to go to Tryon or to Lake Lure, a mountain resort about fifteen miles from Asheville, or else to go see Zelda in Baltimore.

My first thought was the O.K.H.—the Old Kentucky Home, Mrs. Julia Wolfe's rooming house on Spruce Street. I mentioned it to him. His eyes opened wide.

"Take me there," he said, and we rose to go. "Tom and I had a drinking bout in Switzerland when I was there watching over Zelda. We were never so close after that time. Tom expected unqualified admiration for everything, something I couldn't give even to Ernest. I have a critical streak I can't ignore without its going against me."

We walked down the shady, tree-lined street. Before we reached Forty-eight Spruce, I warned him that the Old Kentucky Home was no place for someone living in his style. It was a rambling old house, rundown and dismal, but no worse than the Skyland in Hendersonville where he had taken a dollar room the previous winter. Whether he was serious about staying there, I can't say; he paid little attention to my description of the place and walked on with an unsteady gait.

Fitzgerald slowed down as we neared the grayish wooden structure with the weathered gables and deep front porch. I was the first to go up the worn steps. The bell didn't work; I knocked on the screen door and called, "Mrs. Wolfe." The slight, bony-faced, perky woman appeared in a shabby print dress, stopped abruptly like a bird, and quietly sized us up before opening the screen. I didn't expect her to remember me and she didn't. She gazed with her sharp piercing eyes behind metal-framed glasses, pursed her lips as if undecided, and asked what we wanted in an annoyed and almost commanding voice.

"Mrs. Wolfe, my friend's looking for a room."

"I thought you were insurance salesmen—not folks wanting a room." Her voice and manner suddenly changed; she pushed open the screen and welcomed us inside the cluttered hallway, directing our movements with lively gestures. "More salesmen come knocking than roomers. Times are bad."

"They sure are—"

"Everybody trying to sell something." She spoke fast, paying no attention to me, and pursing her lips in a knowing way. "You wouldn't believe the things they're trying to sell. Only yesterday a boy working his way through college was selling a deodorizer thing for iceboxes. I told him mine didn't stink. I ran him off. I sure did. Humph. I reckon it wasn't friendly of me. As a young woman, I was a book peddler from here to Chimney Rock."

While Mrs. Wolfe spoke she led us into the side porch and then the parlor, volunteering that she could see we had come because of her son Tom. Her mouth was thin-lipped and tight, but it spoke as quick as her sharp eyes and didn't hold back a thing. She pointed to faded family pictures hanging in old gilt frames on the walls. I had seen them before: Tom as a schoolboy and at college, his twin brothers, his sister Mabel, and his father standing before the tombstone shop.

"When I started taking roomers and boarders I had cards printed to drum up trade. But Tom's the best advertising I ever had and cost me nothing. Folks come from everywhere to ask about him." She pursed her lips again and pointed a bony finger at a large, fading picture of the writer as a boy with curls down to his shoulders. "He was my baby. Tom was a bright one. He could talk when he was one and read before he was two. He could read an armful of books between dinner and supper time." She started up the stairs, her lips moving rapidly and without a pause. "I have one room left. Don't take boarders any more. Got no time for them. Only roomers."

I wanted to tell her that my companion was also a writer and a friend of her son. As I began to speak, Fitzgerald nudged me. But it was unnecessary: the birdlike woman chattered on as if she took for granted questions about her son and answered them before we could utter a sound. We exchanged a nod on realizing that she had taken us for a pair of literary tourists.

"Tom's not been in Asheville since his first book came out. I laughed and cried when I read it. What he wrote up about the family was all right with me—as long as he made a success out of it. Some people started calling me Eliza. I didn't get mad. It tickled me." She led us into a room off the upstairs hall. It was gloomy and cluttered, with a large iron bedstead in the center. "But it made plenty folks mad here. Why, they won't even have it in the public library, where he once read every book they had. One day I told Miss Jones, our librarian, it's a shame his books are in all the libraries in the world but his own. She shrugged her shoulders and said Asheville was too poor to buy them. Humph! I know they have them, but under lock and key, and they let only their friends read them. Else how would they know he said those things to make them all sore at him?"

As she walked past the window, the light shone through her thinning gray hair. For a brief moment she was silent; I glanced at Fitzgerald, who was watching her with glassy eyes, fascinated, and yet with an absent look. I wonder whether Mrs. Wolfe, in her forceful eccentricity, reminded him of his own mother. Noticing a film of dust on the old bureau, she brushed it off and then wiped her hand on her dress. With a quick gesture she pushed her spectacles high on her small nose, pursed her lips, and rambled on.

"All my children slept in this room at one time or another—except I reckon Mabel. Mr. Wolfe slept in that little room off the porch downstairs before he passed away. Tom was away at the time." She sighed and put a hand to her flat middle. "Fate's the queerest thing. Mr. Wolfe was a reading man or I might never have met him. It must have been his reading and reciting to Tom that made him want to be a writer. Mr. Wolfe read from Shakespeare and a treasury of prose and poetry. He memorized a lot of fine poetry and used to recite Gray's 'Elegy' to Tom.

"Yes, Tom was born with a liking for reading and writing," she said, raising her hand and heading for the hall. "I believe I could've been a writer myself with a little more education and training. I know a lot about character—after all the folks that passed through this old house. Yes, I was for Tom's becoming one. Mr. Wolfe wanted him to study law. We asked one of our best lawyers what he thought of Tom's chances. He said if Tom had a bent for writing, it had a better future for him. Tom's friend Taylor Bledsoe told him the same thing. Taylor became a lawyer and he's twiddling his thumbs. Too many lawyers. Strange, though; when Tom was a boy, he wanted to be a general."

I had never seen Fitzgerald silent for such a long time. Granted his alcoholic depression, and that Mrs. Wolfe gave nobody a chance, I nevertheless had the feeling that he was overwhelmed by this flood of family lore, echoing all American families that once were, and legendary in the voices that spoke through her.

"For a man who had an eye for the girls, Mr. Wolfe was a good family man. He loved his children and his home. But he was a drinking man." She stopped before a framed picture of Mr. Wolfe hanging in the hallway near the stairs. On hearing her last words Fitzgerald winced and, without her noticing it, fell back against the banister. "It was hard on me. I was a born teetotaler. But it was his vice, not mine. It made a hard woman out of me. When we had words, he called me a cold-hearted woman. I had a sharp tongue, I'll say that. I told him it was his doing—if I was. A tombstone man he was, and he had turned me into a woman of stone."

Mrs. Wolfe went on to speak of the War between the States, saying that many Southern families had never gotten on their feet after it. This was still a deep-running lament in 1935. I later learned that Fitzgerald's father belonged to a well-to-do Baltimore family whose sympathies were with the Confederates; and, like other families after the Civil War, it had become impoverished and ultimately failed in "keeping up appearances."

"Folks ask me if Tom fell in love with any of our boarders." She was now heading down the stairs. "I reckon they ask because Tom wrote about a girl in his book. I don't recall her name offhand. She was older than Tom and engaged back in Virginia. Tom used to take long walks with her. When his sister Mabel made some remark about them, Tom would blush and run out of the house. I told her to stop teasing him. He was about fifteen but tall as a beanpole.

"And everybody wants to know if I had any idea he would be famous," she said, the words coming to us over her slim shoulder as we slowly followed her down the steps. "I had a strong feeling before he was born that he was going to be different from all the rest. I can remember because he was my last. I treated him special, too—after one of the twins died. And some folks want to know if I'm proud of Tom. Of course I am. How else would I be? They look at me and ask if I've changed now that I have a famous son. Humph! I never changed a bit. I go right on running this rooming house. Even if I'm tickled when somebody calls me Eliza, I'll never forgive Tom for calling this 'a bloody barn' in his book. Heh, heh, heh."

The last sounds were a little laugh—the only time she laughed while we were there. We were back at the screen door. I opened it and we stepped out on the porch. She followed and asked if we would take the room. I turned to Fitzgerald, who was leaning against a porch post to steady himself. He wasn't doing a good job; she noticed his shaky movements and sharply grimaced. Her lips shut tight, she pursed them nervously, and then tilted her head proudly.

"I never take drunks—not if I know it."

Mrs. Wolfe opened the screen, walked inside, and slammed it behind her.

We stood there a moment and said nothing. Then I took Fitzgerald by the arm and he slowly followed me down the steps. A hangdog look was on his face. About ten paces away he freed himself and staggered off. He stopped, pursed his lips as she had done, and pointed a shaky finger at the old house.

"Poor Tom! Poor bastard! She's a worse peasant than my mother!"

Molly McQuillan Fitzgerald, as I was to learn from biographies of her son, was a town character of St. Paul as Julia Westall Wolfe was of Asheville. It was said that whatever came into her head popped right out of her mouth. Some called her fey. Some called her a witch-like woman: she carried a black umbrella, rain or shine, wore shoes that didn't match, and read stacks of library books. She adored Scott, who was born after the death of her twin girls in childbirth, and he was to become the pride of her life. As a boy she dressed him up like Little Lord Fauntleroy and made him recite and show off before company, though she took no pains with her own appearance and let her hair fall about her face like a banshee.

Julia Wolfe's flood of family lore had no doubt impressed Fitzgerald by the parallels in Wolfe's parental background and his own. But most striking of all he must have noted that Molly and Julia were both independent and domineering women who had lorded it over their husbands—unbusinesslike men in love with the past. The two women had petted their ambitious sons, who in turn loved their fathers—men doomed to failure who drank more and more, partly to show their contempt for the rising money culture.

────────────12

Fitzgerald was a believer in hunches—call them psychic foresight—and he discussed them with fervent interest. He had hunches about himself, hunches about other people, and hunches about the fate of the world. Many of them were confirmed by events, as notably the hunch about his affair with Rosemary. He had said that it wouldn't be like a well-conceived short story; that it wouldn't run its course through beginning, middle, and end, but instead would be interrupted in the middle. As it happened, the abrupt interruption was a story in itself.

Instead of taking a room at Mrs. Wolfe's rooming house, Fitzgerald went by car to Lake Lure. There he was forlorn and lost, with no one to talk to and share his misery. His eyes clouded with tears, he stared at his unpacked bag, picked up the phone to call Rosemary, and set down the receiver before the operator answered. He wanted to tell Rosemary that he loved her and that her love was necessary to his life.

That night he indulged in the self-pity of an abandoned lover. He drank and sobbed. Sprawled on the bed like a deserted child, he tried to cry himself to sleep. (I remember that he was on the verge of tears when he told me about it some days later at his hotel.) He finally opened his bag, took his combination of pills, had a nightcap, and smoked a final cigarette—his ritual to induce drowsiness. He tossed and turned, perspired, and felt the old burning sensation close to his heart.

He couldn't sleep. That night his imagination worked feverishly. He was playing the jealous lover. Now he tormented himself with pictures of Rosemary in the arms of a man she no longer loved—her husband. How could she, after giving herself to him without reservations? Was it because he hadn't committed himself the way she had done? He had made love to Rosemary shortly before leaving the Inn.

He knew that she wasn't promiscuous, yet he was shocked by the possibility that she could be intimate with two men on the same day.

His tossing and turning could have revived a memory that had rankled in Fitzgerald for a decade. He didn't tell me this, but I thought of it at the time and afterward when I learned more about his life with Zelda. During the first year of their marriage, she had said with her usual insouciance that she could sleep with another man and it wouldn't affect her love for him. He was shocked that she thought so little of fidelity, which meant so much to him. Knowing she was capable of doing whatever she said, he felt from then on that he could never be sure of her.

What he dreaded might happen did take place three years later, when they were living on the Riviera and he was busy finishing *The Great Gatsby*. Whether out of boredom, restlessness, or an impulse to hurt him, or whether because of a genuine infatuation, Zelda became involved with a handsome French aviator. When Fitzgerald realized what was going on, he broke up the friendship with terrible scenes. He considered her act a betrayal of their love and trust; the incident shattered something between them.

Fitzgerald was back from Lake Lure the next day. He took a train North to see Zelda, possibly for her birthday, and then on to New York. I didn't know of his change in plans until after he returned a week later, and he lamented that it was the first time he was too depressed himself to lift Zelda's spirits. He was now staying at the George Vanderbilt, where I had my shop. It was a precaution: he had learned that Rosemary's husband was gone and that she had persuaded him to let her stay on to look after her sister.

There were other reasons for him not to return to the Inn. Determined not to get involved with her again, he thought it unwise to stay in the same hotel; and, if he should be too weak to stick to his resolve and the affair was resumed, he feared that the manager would learn of it from his staff and ask him to leave to protect its reputation as a genteel resort hotel. To maintain his privacy at the George Vanderbilt he registered as Francis Key—the ancestor on his father's side who wrote "The Star-Spangled Banner."

During his absence Rosemary had called his secretary for news of him but had failed to learn where he had gone. She had also written him a half-dozen letters to be forwarded. Her messages overflowed with declarations of passionate love for him. As Fitzgerald read them, his resolve not to see her melted; he called her up, told her that the affair was over, but that he would see her for a little farewell. They drank and dined in his hotel, and the farewell turned out to be a tender reunion.

They were back to where they were before, except that the romance was now more ardent, perhaps because of their separation and the sudden realization that they were together on borrowed time. During the next week Rosemary spent hardly any time with her sister, who scolded her for resuming the affair and neglecting her. Her husband called from time to time to speak with Rosemary, but on most occasions she wasn't at the Inn and he spoke with Myra, who was loyal to her sister and satisfied Ogden with little white lies.

Ogden called one day while Fitzgerald and Rosemary were lunching in the Inn dining room. She picked at her salad while he drank bottles of beer and ale. For the past twenty-four hours she had been trying to convince him that they should go away together and she would support them so he would be free to write his novels. She now spoke of Frieda Lawrence, who had left her husband and children because of her love for her penniless writer. Fitzgerald reminded her that he could never forsake his invalid; and he hedged, telling her that he was used up as a writer, a sick and shattered man.

"Lawrence had weak lungs," he reported her as saying. "They went to sunny places and he wrote about them."

"Lawrence had no fatal flaw like mine."

"I'll help you, darling," she said with her languorous Southern accent.

At a nearby table sat Lottie with an attractive young society woman who was one of her party girls. Lottie was lunching there in the hope of running into Fitzgerald, this time to impress her guest. Her poodles weren't in sight, but *The Great Gatsby* lay on the table. It wasn't lost on Lottie that Fitzgerald was with the prettier of the two sisters, and she was pleased.

Fitzgerald and Lottie exchanged smiles. Rosemary noticed and asked him about the attractive women, but he had no time to reply. A bellboy stepped up to the table and told Rosemary that she was wanted on the phone. It came as a shock to her; Fitzgerald rose and extended his hand to her. As she left the lobby he gave her a reassuring look, despite his own fearful speculation about the call.

The waiter brought more ale and with it a note from Lottie, an invitation to join them if he was free. He picked up his glass and strolled over to their table. Lottie introduced him to her guest who, in spite of her prettiness, appeared dull beside her. The young woman confessed she had never set eyes on an author before.

"They're a breed apart from the human race," Fitzgerald said, with the bravura he summoned up on meeting an impressionable girl. "Never tangle with a writer. Some are vegetarians, some prefer the flesh of their brothers. Many are alcoholics or lonely eccentrics who sit and dream up excitement to compensate for a sedentary life. You can never truly know one. He's too many people trying to be one person—if he's worth a damn as a writer."

"Oh, Mr. Fitzgerald, I'm sure you are!"

"We've been chatting about *Gatsby*—" Lottie pointed to the book. "I was telling Betty Lou how I've read it three times."

Three times? It was Fitzgerald's turn to be flattered, and politely disbelieving. After all, I had told him about her rarely opening a book. But in this case Lottie was candid about the reason for her interest in the novel.

"I was puzzled by the character of Gatsby," she said. "I can't see why such a sweet man—regardless of his shady business—gets himself worked up over such a worthless woman as Daisy. Of course I understand he loves her. But—I hope you don't mind—I think he's a romantic sap in love with a memory."

"He has puzzled others too," he quietly said. He was taken aback by her final remark; it was too close to home. "Yet I believe there are still men left in our society who can feel that way about a woman."

"Do you really?" Lottie asked and quickly added, "You don't have to answer that, Mr. Fitzgerald. But I haven't seen you lately. You've been away?"

"Quite a bit. I've lost your number. Where are Romeo and Juliet?"

"Juliet and Romeo," she corrected with a smile and jotted down a number on the corner of the menu. "They're being groomed at the Canine Château."

As she handed him the number of the dog salon, Fitzgerald noticed Rosemary staring at him from the doorway. He excused himself and went toward her. Rosemary showed signs of shock; she was rigid and very pale. Suddenly she turned and rushed out. He stopped and then started after her, slowly but anxiously.

The call had been from Myra; it was prompted by one from Rosemary's husband in Memphis. Ogden had phoned for her, Myra again lied to him. But this was the last time, Myra cried, that she would lie "to that decent man." She sounded hysterical, going over old ground with her sister—"behaving like a hussy with your has-been lover"—and saying that next time she would tell Ogden the truth.

But Rosemary was no more discreet about her affair, nor did she

spend more time with her sister to placate her. The threat, if anything, seemed to have induced in her a more willful and reckless behavior. Fitzgerald was no help to Rosemary, with his drinking and
longing to have her with him. Alone and forsaken, Myra stepped up
her own drinking; she took more sleeping pills and was often in tears.
In time her crying jag led to a bad case of hysterics.

The jolt that brought Rosemary to her senses came one morning
soon afterward. Bellboys found Myra sprawled on the Inn golf
course, drugged, drunk, and sound asleep. Fitzgerald got a nurse to
look after her, Rosemary arranged to move out of the Inn—possibly at
the request of the manager—and took rooms at the Battery Park
Hotel. It was downtown, facing Grove Arcade, where I worked for
Lamar Stringfield, and a block or so from the George Vanderbilt.

After they settled there, Rosemary did something in her panicky
state which Fitzgerald said was to bring about the sudden interruption
of their romance. He was ready to call a local doctor or psychiatrist
for Myra, but Rosemary insisted on phoning their family doctor in
Memphis. The doctor had known them since birth; she begged him to
fly up and take charge of her sister. The doctor agreed and called her
husband. Within minutes Ogden phoned to tell her that he was bringing the doctor there in a chartered plane.

Shortly after his arrival the family doctor, in whom the girls had
always confided, learned that he had two patients on his hands, and
the one who most needed him at the moment was Rosemary. After
giving them both a sedative, he contacted Fitzgerald, who was eager
to see him and recommend a New York psychiatrist for Myra. But
the doctor was more interested in his affair with Rosemary: if it were
to continue, Fitzgerald reported him as saying, it would mean disaster
for all of them.

The doctor had already planned the return of the sisters to Memphis. He was to fly back with Myra, Rosemary was to motor home
with her husband. There were to be no farewells. Fitzgerald was to
make no attempts to see or call Rosemary; and the doctor would see to
it that she didn't call or try to see him. Later, if Fitzgerald cared to
know about her, he could reach her through his office. But at the
moment Rosemary could take no more excitement; it would be too
much for her jangled nerves. The doctor was confident that it was the
only way for Rosemary to resume her life with the handsome and understanding husband who worshiped her.

Though Fitzgerald's emotions were deeply tangled with Rosemary,
he grasped the doctor's logic and agreed to do as he was told. In a

way, he was relieved to have the affair interrupted by an outside force; neither he nor Rosemary was capable of going on or of bringing their relation to a satisfactory end. When Fitzgerald left the white-haired doctor, he told me that he had taken a deep breath, as if he had just missed being hit by a truck while blindly crossing a busy street.

It was Rosemary who was too shattered to do as her doctor warned. She called Fitzgerald to tell him that Ogden was taking her home. She didn't want to go back with him. If Fitzgerald loved her, now was the time to show it and keep her there. Of course he loved her, he tried to assure her, but he had promised her doctor to give her up—to prevent a family disaster.

Rosemary cried, begged, and pleaded, saying that if he let her go, she would kill herself. Though the threat was to haunt him later, his present turmoil kept him from being sensitive to the state of her mind or emotions. Fitzgerald said he hung up, threw his things in a bag, and phoned for a bellboy. Twenty minutes later he was out of the Vanderbilt—without giving a thought to where he was going this time.

13

I didn't see or hear from him for about ten days. He telephoned me one morning to say that he was back in town, after an unexpected trip North; that everything had happened while he was away, and that he was feeling the worse for it. He invited me over to his new hotel, the Battery Park, told me his room number, and warned me that he was registered as Anthony Blaine. The name was a combination of Anthony Patch and Amory Blaine, heroes of his two early novels and fictional portraits of himself. At the moment, he was more like the doomed Patch than the eager and effervescent Blaine.

Compared with Grove Park Inn, the hotel was of the commercial kind like one of the Statler or Hilton chain. He had a rather small room with English fox-hunt prints on the walls and appeared out of place in it. The setting seemed to emphasize his pallor and low spirits; he was drinking and his hands trembled, while his mind raced on turbulently. He spoke with an increasing intensity and in an apocalyptic vein, mingling references to worldwide disaster and his personal fate as though one grew out of the other.

"I have a hunch—a sixth sense—about the way things are going in this mutable world," I recall his saying, in the manner of a trained actor. "You might call me a barometer. Our civilization is doomed. It may not survive another decade or two. The war brought on the newly rich and an extravagant era of excesses and middle-class vulgarities, probably the most vulgar of all the gilded ages.

"The Boom spawned the Bust, bringing in its wake misery, economic chaos, and a plague on everything spiritual. I see no future in either prayer or science—where is the spirit in science? God knows there's no future in capitalism's rotten profit system, and I have no faith in the future of my kind in the supposedly classless society.

We're finished, done for, doomed."

Although I realized he meant everything he was saying, there was a double edge to it. This was more than *Weltschmerz*. I waited and he got to the point. It was over with Rosemary—it was finished for good this time. But he was overcome by a sense of loss, shame, and self-hatred for having let her go. She had loved him and risked everything, while he had simply drifted along with her. Yes, she had ruined it all with that call, yet he had let her go and left her to pick up the pieces of a shattered marriage.

He mourned her and was filled with remorse. Well, he was a coward, he told me. Which was to say, there were things in himself and situations he couldn't cope with. It was nothing new, though; he had behaved that way on other important occasions in his life. He had learned to live with this incapacity, as he called it. He had tried to balance it with certain willful acts—acts that proved more foolhardy than courageous. But the world was full of cowards, he said, without trying to console himself. History was run on that basis. That, and stupidity.

He was pacing from one window to the other in the small room, his speech and movements flowing in a rhythm that came from long practice at dictating to secretaries. He paused before one of the lifeless fox-hunt prints, staring at it without seeing it, and turned back to me.

"Doom. One final smash. No tears. We must not try to stop it. This is the natural law. Birth, flowering, and decline. The curve of personal and world history." As he spoke he gave his wrist a deft turn, drawing a curve with his lighted cigarette. "This is history. Historical perspective. The rise and fall of leaders, world powers, cultures, and civilizations. We Americans can control the destiny of the world, yet we are helpless. We have no workable economic plan or mature culture to save us from destruction."

He brooded a moment and returned to Rosemary. While he was away, Fitzgerald said, he had kept in touch with his secretary; she had told him of Rosemary's desperate calls along the way to Memphis. She kept saying she loved him, and then dashed off passionate letters to him. The morning Scott got back he received one saying she had tried to kill herself with an overdose of pills soon after reaching home. Fortunately she was rushed to the hospital and saved.

There was no way to reach her except through her doctor and Fitzgerald couldn't be sure she would get a message from him. He had sent her a tender wire, speaking of his love for her and how much she had meant to him. That was followed by a letter in a more restrained tone, reminding her of their duty to those whom they loved prior to their meeting. Also that his present situation was hopeless. So hopeless that he was unworthy of her love and youth, and that he could serve no purpose whatsoever in her life.

There was a short silence while Fitzgerald went to the highboy for another drink. As the time passed, his manner had undergone a change. His gestures became jerky. His bright eyes dulled and looked incipiently menacing, his voice coarsened. Although he gradually lost his actor's poise and delivery, his thoughts were as volatile as ever. He veered away abruptly from the subject of Rosemary, pacing the small room and expounding his ideas with an urgency that seemed to be insisting on his fundamental worth, as though he were digging back, so to speak, to permanent values.

Oswald Spengler and Karl Marx were the only modern thinkers who had any meaning today, he declared. Marx had helped to form his own class-consciousness and influenced some of his best writing, while Spengler's *Decline of the West*, stressing upper-class attitudes and the power of money in contemporary culture, had deepened his romantic skepticism. He had started reading Spengler in 1927, and he called *Decline* his "bed book."

"I'm still under its spell," he said. "Probably I shall never get over it."

He remembered being interviewed by a New York reporter some years before who couldn't believe that the spokesman and legendary figure of the irresponsibly gay Jazz Age had turned pessimist in so short a time. Fitzgerald snorted. He had given the fellow a piece of his mind, pointing out that his early novels were steeped in skepticism and open to despair—the touchstone of youth, quick to an affinity with Dostoevski (as shortly a generation saw itself in T. S. Eliot's poem "The Hollow Men").

"It wasn't Spengler who introduced me to this outlook, but Mencken in his early essays. They had a hell of an impact on me. Some of his ideas found their way into *The Beautiful and Damned*. But it's Spengler's skepticism that sticks with me as the logical philosophical position of our time. A philosopher who stands on the shoulders of Nietzsche—whose ideas I first met in Mencken—and Nietzsche on the shoulders of Goethe. Goethe—"

Suddenly he crossed the room toward me, pulling a letter from his pocket. He fumbled with it, unfolding it, saying something about the comment I had made on the difference between his handwriting and Faulkner's. I understood immediately that the letter was from Rosemary. He spoke of her attempted suicide, and he speculated on the possibility that she might try again and succeed. He seemed to be asking me, without putting it into words, to examine her handwriting.

I took the letter and studied the formation of the letters. The handwriting showed signs of being erratic and somewhat unbalanced, but it was on the whole, I thought, too vital and earthbound to indicate self-destruction.

"How do you know?" he asked hoarsely. He sat down close to me and gazed at me with troubled eyes. "I thought so myself, but I can't be sure. Are you?"

"I don't know enough to be that sure," I answered. "I know more about hands. I'm learning handwriting. They're related but hands tell us more."

Fitzgerald was studying his own hands. They were pale as usual and shaky; he tried to control them and cursed under his breath. I turned to the letter for another look. On the last page I noticed a name that wasn't Rosemary's. Fitzgerald was talking about palmistry, that he believed in it, how his Dollar Woman had given him an intelligent reading, and that he never tired of having his hands read. They were open before me—an invitation.

But I was interested in the signature on the letter. I pointed to the name and looked at him with a puzzled smile. He grimaced and snatched it from me, rose, and went to the highboy. He told me to forget what I saw, made himself another drink, and was silent for a long moment.

He had called her Rosemary, he finally said, not to protect her, but because her youthful spirit and beauty had reminded him of the character in *Tender Is the Night* and the young Hollywood actress he had used as the model for the fictional Rosemary. But that wasn't all. He pointed out that her given name was similar to that of a principal character in another of his novels; the two women had nothing in common, reinforcing his disinclination to call "Rosemary" by her own name.

"Do you by any chance know this young woman?"

"No."

"Good." He was silent again. "It probably appealed to my writer's instinct to name her after one of my characters. The one she most resembled," he said with a lordly gesture. "Although most of what I've told you is fact, I did take liberties. The sort I take when I turn a personal experience into fiction. I was telling you what I may some day get a chapter out of. Or a story. I didn't intend to deceive you.

There's a decided kinship between fiction and reality as a situation takes shape in the writing. . . ."

Fitzgerald was now drunk. He wavered and slumped in a chair before me and rubbed his trembling, well-shaped hands. I glanced from him to the small room and asked him why he was there instead of at the Inn. He said he couldn't go there, at least not for a day or two. It was a question of money and too many memories. Moreover, he needed to pull himself together, wherever he was, before he could do any writing.

"My heart's dead, now that she's gone. She saved me for a while. I found something of my youth with her, and some of my old vitality. There seemed to be a future for me. At times I knew it was only a mirage, but there were moments when it was radiantly real. Now that's all behind me. Youth, vitality, and something of a future. I've been in the dumps before; it's a hard uphill road. But depression becomes deeper as the years pass and the uphill pull gets harder. Probably I'm getting ready for the end."

He was quiet for a long time; I said nothing. I remember my saying nothing because of the hateful look he suddenly gave me.

"Christ, how can you stand me!"

I sat back. My silence and apparent indifference seemed to increase his hostility toward me. In fact, I didn't know how to handle this situation any more than those in life from which he had begged off.

He grimaced, looking sideways at me, then rose unsteadily and lunged toward the highboy. A bottle fell to the carpeted floor, a glass crashed at his feet. I jumped up and started toward him; he motioned me away. I stood there, weary and uncomfortable, quite aware that he was on his way to a violent drunk.

It was something I didn't care to stick around for. I moved toward the door again. Now he came after me. He took me by the arm and forced me back into the chair. Then he sat down stiffly opposite me and thrust forward his trembling big hands.

"Go on, you bastard!" he said in his meanest tone. "Tell me the worst!"

For that time I managed to change the subject.

14

By August the Intimate Bookshop had also become a meeting place of the socially committed young people, drawn mainly from colleges, who represented an active minority in that conservative Southern state. They were interested in literature and serious nonfiction, sometimes bought a book on credit, and sat around talking, smoking, and drinking coffee. Their visits were a welcome relief from our regular clientele—the cash customers who kept our bookshop open.

One afternoon Fitzgerald walked in when Phil Russel—not Phillips Russell, but a younger man—Bill Buttrick, and I were arguing about the use of revolutionary tactics for the preservation of peace (a subject that is not the discovery of the current generation). Fitzgerald was freshly shaven, sober, and in low spirits; seeing the young group, he started to retreat, but I drew him back inside and introduced him to my friends. I knew he felt out of touch with the younger generation, but he agreed to stay, provided we went on with our discussion. He said it reminded him of bull sessions in his early Princeton days, and later in the back room of the Kilmarnock Book Shop in St. Paul, while he was working on his first two novels.

Fitzgerald was soon drawn into the conversation and supported the liberal position held by Bill, which at the moment was losing out to Phil's radicalism. Phil, whom I remember as stocky, red-haired, and full of vigor, spoke with the brilliance and conviction that had won him top honors in Chapel Hill debating circles. Bill, a semi-invalid with a frail build, was slow of speech but was just as logical and earnest in his argument. Seeing that Bill was no match for Phil's fire, Fitzgerald came to his rescue. His voice began to sound in the small shop, his spirits obviously getting a boost as he held his own with the robust student.

Yet it appeared that he was more interested in Phil and Bill as bright, articulate, politically oriented youths of the Depression generation than in the subject itself, and the more he talked, the more his opinions took on a conservative tone. Phil was on top of him quickly, reminding him of a passage near the end of *This Side of Paradise* in which Amory says that he was "a product of a versatile mind in a restless generation—with every reason to throw my mind and pen in with the radicals."

"Yes, I was a rebel and I haven't stopped being one," Fitzgerald said. "But I also have Amory saying that he and his kind would struggle against tradition, and try to displace old cants with new ones. Like Amory, I used to think I was right about life, but such faith is difficult to sustain, and disillusionment comes soon enough to bury old ambitions and unrealized dreams."

"You ended that novel already sounding disillusioned," Phil said. He threw back his head, half shutting his eyes, and recalled the words he wanted. "You spoke of the past hovering over your generation, a new generation raised on old beliefs and shouting the old cries, but 'dedicated more than the last to the fear of poverty and the worship of success; grown up to find all Gods dead, all wars fought, all faiths in man shaken.' I remember those lines. I quoted them in a recent debate on peace, comparing your so-called lost generation with ours."

"Gertrude Stein tagged us," Fitzgerald said a little apologetically. "It stuck and colored our outlook and manner. But cynicism was a face-saving device for us when we saw through the grandiose lies. It's your generation that is inheriting the final consequences of those lies—a ruin all around you. How did you use my lines?"

"In not too complimentary a fashion, Mr. Fitzgerald," Phil answered with an aplomb that should have reminded Fitzgerald of his own cocky youth. "I used them as a warning against defeatism, against the notion that it's all over but the burial. I pointed out that the old gods were false, the old faiths opiates, and that war itself was around the corner. If we didn't want it, we had to do something drastic and quick to save world freedom and peace instead of helping to build up the new war machines of Hitler, Mussolini, and Japan. And the answer to fear and poverty was to work to end the exploitation of all human and natural resources solely for the God-almighty dollar."

"I agree in principle, but your words have a familiar ring." Fitzgerald gave me a discreetly knowing glance. "Where did you say this—at Chapel Hill?"

"There, and at a Students' International Peace Conference in Switzerland."

I served coffee. While we drank it, Fitzgerald turned to Bill, who had been out of the conversation during this last round, asking him questions about his background and whether he was going into politics. Bill explained that his field was social work. After a term at the new, experimental Black Mountain College nearby, he was now teaching at Commonwealth College in Mena, Arkansas. This was a workers' school in the Ozarks, where there was perhaps more ingrained poverty and ignorance than in any other rural area in the country. The work there consisted of showing the mountain folk how to improve their lot through education, small cooperatives, and union organization.

"The property owners and storekeepers don't like us," Bill said with a laugh. "They're trying to scare us off by saying we're free-loving, Christ-hating radicals from way up North. One of us is Jewish, but they'd say we were anyhow. Now they're after the state politicians to get rid of us. If that doesn't work, I reckon they'll try the sheriff. He's one of them."

"I wouldn't be surprised," Scott nodded. "Is there any poverty here?"

Phil was the one to answer. "Where the tourists can't see it, Mr. Fitzgerald. The people in these mountains survive on wild animals and herbs. The only cash they see is what their kids can get picking galax, those waxy green leaves used in funeral decorations."

Then Phil told Fitzgerald about another side of Asheville life. Behind its serene façade of misty mountains and the rhododendron festival, a press was rolling out millions of copies of pamphlets, flyers, and books vilifying Catholics, Jews, Negroes, labor unions, the foreign-born, and, with special venom, President Roosevelt for his recognition of the Soviet Union. This was the Galahad Press, sponsored by the Silver Shirts of America, an organization with insignia, uniforms, and salute that openly imitated the Nazis.

The founder and spokesman of the Silver Shirts, with headquarters in Asheville, was William Dudley Pelley, a retired U.S. Army general whose appearance would have met Hollywood's ideal for active duty. Dressed in a tailor-made gray uniform, Pelley directed Silver Shirt activities from his office there, and traveled the country addressing clubs and rallies of fearful, one-hundred-per-cent Americans.

"I'd like to get a look at him," Fitzgerald remarked scornfully.

"His office isn't far from here."

But Fitzgerald didn't see Phil again, and while I could have arranged for him to meet Pelley, having interviewed the man at one of his local meetings, Fitzgerald never spoke to me about him.

He stayed after the two students left. He was struck by the difference between them and the friends who had frequented the St. Paul bookshop. That circle had been purely literary; its members discussed poetry and fiction, and there were one or two novels under way. Politics and the world situation seemed not to exist for them. They were absorbed in literary ambitions, each with the dream of achieving success.

"While I was writing *Paradise* I saw a lot of Donald Ogden Stewart, though he wasn't part of that crowd," Fitzgerald said, pacing the shop now that he had it to himself. "He was from the East and was Ernest's model for Bill Gorton in *The Sun*. He had come to Minneapolis working for an insurance company, I believe, and we spent evenings talking about Shaw, Wells, Mencken, Upton Sinclair, and Havelock Ellis. Don has a literary gift, a critical mind, and an engaging humor. We both sold our first stuff to *The Smart Set*. He was helpful in shaping up *Paradise*. We didn't meet in the bookstore but at a dance in St. Paul. I remember him leading a cotillion. I loved to dance in those days."

He passed on to talk about Peggy and Tom Boyd, the mainstays of the bookshop, who were to become his close friends. Peggy was writing stories and later published a highly regarded collection of them. Tom also wrote, although he had his hands full as part owner of the Kilmarnock and book editor of the St. Paul *Daily News*. It was Tom who interviewed Fitzgerald after the success of *This Side of Paradise* and called him "St. Paul's only famous author." At the time, Tom had written a novel about World War I, *Through the Wheat*, which Scribners had rejected; later they published it solely because of Fitzgerald's enthusiasm. The book received excellent reviews and enjoyed a fair success.

"Your friend Phil reminds me of Tom. The same assurance and vitality, the same easy flow of expression, and the kind of dedication that was to ruin Tom a few years later." He stopped and gave me a pointed look. "Qualities that go with the talented young. I don't say your friend has talent—or you—but Tom had more than his share. I admired his novel, but I didn't have the same faith in him that I had in Ernest and Cummings. The limitations in Tom took over when he quit writing about what he knew and turned out phony American peasant stuff. We never had the kind of peasants you read about in books about old Russia, but the critics ate it up as genuine—the same critics who later ignored me for writing about trivial people, the socially insignificant rich."

Boyd ruined himself that way, Fitzgerald lamented. His estimation of Boyd's work hit bottom with the publication a few years later of *Samuel Drummond*. The book angered Fitzgerald because its one-dimensional characters were presented as the salt of the earth. His prediction that the book wouldn't sell, but would be dead in a month, proved right. At the time, Fitzgerald worried about Boyd and was anxious to see him, fearing he would become embittered by failure. (I later noticed that he wrote to Perkins about Boyd in this regard.) Then a few years later, Boyd seemed to have dropped out of the literary scene.

"The tragedy is that Tom had a strong talent. *Through the Wheat* was one of our best war novels, along with *Three Soldiers* and *The Enormous Room*. This was before the war became a popular subject in plays and films. Then Stallings made a fortune out of *What Price Glory?* I honestly believe Stallings could never have written it without having read Tom's book—just as Kaufman could never have written *Of Thee I Sing* without having absorbed the idea from my comedy, *The Vegetable*. When *What Price Glory?* was going to be filmed, Stallings referred the producer to Tom's book for background material. It was a case of Tom and I creating something original and somebody else making it slick and obvious."

Fitzgerald had heard conflicting stories about what had happened to Boyd in recent years. He wanted to know whether I had any news of him. It happened that a month or so earlier I had read of Boyd's sudden death the previous January. This came as no shock to Scott, but his face sagged, taking on an aged look. The news was in a tribute to Boyd by the critic Granville Hicks, delivered at the American Writers' Congress in New York City that April.

Hicks said that Boyd had been "searching for a fundamental understanding of American life," and that he didn't find it until he had allied himself with the working class. Boyd had joined the Communist Party in Vermont and had worked actively for it, writing the while. In the fall of 1934, Boyd became a candidate for governor of the state on the Communist ticket. The following January he died, but Hicks' piece didn't mention the cause of his death.

"The poor bastard," Fitzgerald said softly. "He went haywire."

There was no difference, after all, between my friends and his own,

Fitzgerald remarked. His friends may have started out as literary in St. Paul, Princeton, or elsewhere, but those who amounted to anything had eventually taken the left fork of the road. Fitzgerald hadn't gone along, I knew well enough by now, but at this time I felt he was experiencing a peculiar sensation, a stance temporarily outside of his personal reservations. He was seeing the political face of his time much as one sees a face in modern art—one face, all faces, an abstraction that holds the reality.

Then Boyd's name reminded him of something, an association on the surface of the mind that didn't distract him from his contemplation of the road taken by most of his friends. He asked whether I had met James Boyd of Southern Pines or Margaret Culkin Banning of Tryon, who belonged to the horse-and-hounds set.

"No, but I've reviewed their books," I answered, willing to change the subject for his sake. "One writer I do know is Olive Tilford Dargan, who has turned novelist under the name of Fielding Burke. She lives here in West Asheville and her novel is *Call Home the Heart*. I think it is"—he wasn't paying much attention to what I said, but I struggled on—"why, it seems to me as poetic and honest in dealing with her Carolina mountain people as Mary Webb's *Precious Bane* in its English country setting. Dargan started as a poet and she was published by Scribners too. I'm to interview her after the Southern Writers' Conference at Black Mountain this month."

By now Fitzgerald was slumped in the chair, his face buried in his hands. In a voice that carried emotion he murmured, "That clever kid. He ran the best book page west of New York . . . the poor son of a bitch."

15

Still, Fitzgerald must have heard what I said about interviewing Fielding Burke, and must have remembered, too, that he had mentioned his "generations" idea as a possible story for my newspaper. He phoned in the end of August and apologized for not having done something about it sooner, considering that the interview might bring me a little cash. He blamed it not on a bad memory or his lack of concern for my fortunes, but on his poor physical condition and the disturbing nature of the Rosemary affair.

The affair was over, he assured me, but he and Rosemary were now caught up in its aftereffects. She kept writing him pitiful love letters which were more upsetting than flattering to him. He wrote her that she was better off with her husband, but found he couldn't dissuade her from believing that the separation was temporary. Rosemary again tried to take her life. This time, however, he conceded that her attempts would all be failures. Instead of worrying about her, he mourned his loss of her on lonely nights when too much beer led to a crying jag.

His soft voice brightened when he asked whether Lottie was in town—and had I seen her? It was why he had dropped by the bookshop; it had slipped his mind after joining the discussion with my friends. I hadn't seen her for about a week, and that meant she was out of town. He asked if I believed her claim that she had read *Gatsby* three times. I said that she had never lied to me. He then invited me to his suite—by that time he was back at Grove Park Inn—for lunch and the interview.

When I stepped off the elevator I found him waiting at his door to greet me. This struck me as a bit odd; he had never done it before. He was dressed in fashionable sports clothes and the room was tidy, with

an air of formality about him and his quarters. His manner was courteous, cordial instead of friendly, and with almost none of the old intimacy. Though under control, he appeared to be keyed up like an
actor about to make his entrance on opening night. Puzzled by the
change, I dropped my habitual informality and turned into a reporter.
He was quick to notice this and spoke without meeting my eyes, so
that he seemed all the more distant.

"This is probably my first interview in eight years," he said, in-
dicating a chair for me to sit in. "As you may know, I took an awful
licking from some writers. This could be the real reason why I didn't
have you sooner for it."

"Yes, I—" I didn't finish the sentence as I sat down to face him. I
wanted to say that he didn't have to fear me, he could be more relaxed
about it. After all, I was a friend and on his side.

There must have been a cache of beer bottles in his bedroom. He
disappeared there for a moment and emerged with a foaming glass.
He asked me if I would join him and wasn't surprised when I said I
would have some with lunch. That reminded him to call for a menu;
he picked up the phone, spoke to room service, and lit a cigarette.

With the cigarette in one hand and the glass in the other, taking
slow, thoughtful steps, Fitzgerald paced the big light-filled room. He
drank and smoked, gestured with the graceful movements of a dancer,
and held forth on his favorite subject—writers. He spoke with a swag-
ger of confidence and ease, as if his ideas flowed from an inexhaustible
fountain. When he noticed me scribbling on an envelope, he stopped
abruptly.

"Don't quote me directly," he said in a formal tone that he maintained through most of the visit. "I write better than I talk."

I slipped the envelope and the pencil into my pocket. Perhaps he
was being modest, but that August day I took him at his word, and
for some reason I began to feel in awe of him as I had never felt
before—and had never felt of, Faulkner, Anderson, Dreiser, Lewis,
or any of the other writers I had met or interviewed.

The glass empty, he vanished into the other room, refilled it, and
came back to hold forth on Nietzsche, Henri Bergson, Thorstein
Veblen, and Henry George, with a reference here and there to Marx
and Spengler. Then he settled down to the novelists again, those of
his era, and acknowledged their influence on him, if not always praising their work. It seemed, at times, that he was trying out ideas he
might later use in print.

He kept on drinking. His actor's voice rose abruptly and sounded scornful as he launched into comments on the then fashionable, but to him shoddy stuff—proletarian literature. He was combative about it and sure of himself, saying that it was contrived, derivative of European masters, insincere and unimaginative, and a waste of material.

He stopped when the waiter brought the menus. Handing one of them to me, he told the smiling Negro to bring him his usual light lunch. After the waiter left, Fitzgerald said the Negro was a musician, and then dashed back into the other room for a quick refill. I noticed his first trips, but lost count after seven or eight.

"We Americans are wasting our literary resources as fast as everything else," he said. He lit another cigarette and told me of an article he had written on the subject some years ago for *The Bookman*. In that piece he had placed most of the blame on Sherwood Anderson. While others called Anderson an inarticulate writer bursting with ideas, Fitzgerald said he was one of our finest prose stylists with no ideas at all. "Anderson's crime was influencing some young writers to turn out mediocre, half-baked books, without the style or feeling to give them depth and life."

He sat down for a moment on the couch facing me and spoke of writers he still admired: Flaubert, Anatole France, Dickens, Thackeray, Shaw, and Conrad—all masters of their craft. Americans who had left their mark on him included Frank Norris, Mark Twain, Henry James, Dreiser, Upton Sinclair, and Mencken. Some helped to shape his iconoclastic thinking, others his skeptical and pessimistic outlook.

After another quick refill he bounced back, paced before me, and spoke about his contemporaries. Three had figured prominently in his life and work. First there was John Peale Bishop, whom he had met as a freshman at Princeton. Bishop introduced him to the Elizabethans and the English Romantic poets, Keats among them. These led Fitzgerald to the French Symbolists, who were to stimulate the poetic imagery of his work.

"It was probably the poet in us," he said, "that held us together despite our personal differences."

Then he spoke of the second, Edmund Wilson, whom he described as an intellect "packed with cerebral energy." He said that Wilson tried writing novels, but his mind was of the analytic, critical kind. When they met at Princeton, Fitzgerald claimed that he was more of a rebel than Wilson was, though Wilson had since turned to economics and political history. In his recent book, *The American Jitters*, he had written about the collapse of capitalism.

"Our depression has led Bunny into the communist camp. He's now in the Soviet Union and seems favorably impressed. For a long time I've thought of Bunny as my intellectual conscience." (When I asked Wilson some years later what Fitzgerald could have meant by this, he replied in part, "I think that my role as his intellectual conscience has consisted mainly in lending and suggesting books to him to read from time to time.")

Fitzgerald emptied his glass and went to open another bottle. When he came back, he spoke about the third—Ernest Hemingway. I later learned that they had met in Paris in 1925, shortly after Fitzgerald published *The Great Gatsby;* it was a time for him of "a thousand parties and no work." Hemingway, three years his junior, had abandoned journalism to make it as a writer. His stories were appearing in little magazines and limited avant-garde editions while Fitzgerald's were earning him thousands in *The Saturday Evening Post.*

"It was a frightful inducement to write for money and I had good reason." He stopped to open the door for the waiter. "I thought you were my secretary," he said. "She should be here in a minute."

While the waiter set up a table, Fitzgerald turned back to me. "She's bringing a snapshot she took of me in front of her garage. The only photo I have. I hope it will do."

"Something candid to go with the interview."

"It's candid, and I'm standing on my own two feet," he said, without smiling at his own joke. He returned to his earlier subject when the waiter left us, saying he had buried his dream of becoming "the best damned writer" because of necessity and his facility for cheapness. "But they were honest stories, even if they had the look of formula magazine stuff."

He said he did all he could to help Hemingway because of his unqualified respect for Hemingway's talent as a dedicated writer. In that *Bookman* piece he mentioned, Fitzgerald had spoken of his friend as the new hope of American letters. He had steered him to Max Perkins at Scribners, knowing he would be in good hands. Admiring him as a friend and artist, he considered Hemingway his "artistic conscience."

But Hemingway's success with *The Sun Also Rises* and *A Farewell to Arms* had brought a change in their friendship, he remarked in a personal aside. He admitted Hemingway was a genius, but said that he himself was "a plodder" in his serious work; and though he sounded as anxious to maintain his top position as Hemingway had no doubt been anxious to replace him, Fitzgerald reminded me that he had been silent as a serious writer during the nine years between *The Great Gatsby* and *Tender Is the Night*.

"You have to be careful whom you do favors for," he said, going for another glass of beer. The buzzer sounded, he went to open the door. "Come in, dear. I thought it was the waiter with our lunch. I take it you've eaten."

"Yes, I have."

I rose to greet his ladylike secretary, whom I remembered as his Dollar Woman. She sat near me and, for the moment, refused a drink. Fitzgerald went on speaking about Hemingway, saying he had remained loyal and devoted to him, though Ernest had criticized him personally and professionally. It seemed to me that Fitzgerald worshiped Hemingway for qualities he lacked in himself and had endowed him with, as one does with a hero or beloved woman.

He was getting another beer when the waiter rolled in our lunch on a dolly. I sat before a roast-beef sandwich and a salad; Fitzgerald his usual bowl of soup with crackers. His Dollar Woman sat off to the side; she had come to take dictation from him and also to bring me the photo. While Fitzgerald nibbled the crackers and sipped a few spoonsful of soup, he spoke of the six generations that had appeared since World War I. I jotted down a key word here and there, mostly listened, and barely touched my food for fear of missing something he was saying.

"Yes, we were brought up that way," his Dollar Woman interrupted, as he described her prewar generation.

Sharply turning on her, he said, "Don't interrupt me or try to put words in my mouth. I've given them a lot of thought. Part of your great charm is your silence."

She sat back and wasn't heard from again while I was there. When he finished, she handed me the snapshot, and I left the Inn dazed by the three-hour monologue. I had sat there like a statue and not asked a single question. My head was full of ideas and impressions, but I didn't have more than fifty key words on the envelope. They were ample. Two days later I wrote the piece; it appeared in the Raleigh *News and Observer*, September 1, 1935. Here is a summary:

Fitzgerald's six generations are Pre-War, War, Post-War, Boom, Shock, and Hard Times. He made a point of saying that the first three centered around the war and its effects, the others around the booming twenties and the Depression of the thirties; and he mentioned a book that best typified each generation and its era.

He said that the Pre-War generation was strongly attached to the Victorian tradition and, that, although it fancied itself modern, it was inhibited and basically moralistic in ideas and behavior. The novel he chose to best describe it was H. G. Wells's *Ann Veronica*.

Of the War generation, he declared that plenty had been said about it, but that the best was Hemingway's remark, "The words duty, honor, and courage lost all reality, and only things seemed to have any dignity . . . names of places, mountains, and rivers." *A Farewell to Arms* was his choice for the lost generation book. (The exact words in the novel are "Abstract words such as glory, honor, courage . . . were obscene beside the concrete names of villages, the numbers of roads, and the names of rivers.")

The Post-War generation was a disrupted one, weak and inclined to seek guidance from the older groups. He found no vitality in this generation and said it was best described by such novels as Percy Marks's *The Plastic Age* and *Flaming Youth*, which Samuel Hopkins Adams wrote under the name of Warner Fabian.

The Boom generation was "brassy, metallic, and its ethics were unsympathetic. The best quality was a scorn of weakness, its worst a sort of inhumanity." It was conditioned by parental optimism that boomed, "Maybe in five years I'll own the company!" Peter Arno's *Hullabaloo* was the book for this generation.

Fitzgerald said that the Shock generation was similar to that of the war and the generation that grew up under defeat in the South after the Civil War: "The blow gave it dignity." It was prematurely old, daring, and unhappy, but he said it would prove itself more worthy of respect than the two preceding generations. Faulkner's *Pylon* was his choice as a morbid representation of the Shock era.

The youngest generation was that of Hard Times. He thought the less that parents tried to influence their children, the more effective they could be in making them believe in a few old truths such as honor, duty, courage, honesty. In his opinion, the novel that best captured the Depression generation had yet to be written.

I later learned that he had told his Dollar Woman I would receive fifty dollars for this story. Probably he was trying to impress her or boost his own morale in those troubled days when he was getting two hundred dollars instead of four thousand for his stories. I never told him, but I confided to her that I was paid at space rates—ten cents an inch—and got the grand sum of three dollars for the interview. Or, at least, that is what she wrote in her diary, which appeared in *Esquire*.

Reading the interview some twenty years later, I felt that it was bare and dull. That day's enchantment eluded me. None of his glowing words had gotten into it. Perhaps it was his warning me not to quote him—it froze up my memory. Yet his performance before me as a member of the press still remains fixed in my mind as the one-man show of an Olympian. And, to this day, I think that effect was what he wanted to produce.

16

A few days after the interview Fitzgerald asked me how I had gotten that long letter from Bernard Shaw in 1932, and what had led to its being reprinted on the dust jacket of Dr. Archibald Henderson's "authorized" biography, *Bernard Shaw: Playboy and Prophet.* He was curious to know why Shaw had chosen "this obscure math prof at the University of North Carolina to become his Boswell."

As early as the fall of 1931 in Chapel Hill, all of us at *Contempo* had been puzzled by the choice and thought it would make a good story for the magazine. We didn't follow up on it until the day Professor Henderson, a Victorian gentleman who had a high forehead and wore high celluloid collars, first breezed into our bookshop there. But before we could ask him, he had chosen an armful of mystery novels from our rental shelf, plunked down his dollar deposit, and floated down the campus street like a kid who had stumbled on a treasure.

Keeping the professor in the latest thrillers, I told Fitzgerald, was like Scheherazade dreaming up new tales to save her head. During a weekend of relaxation reading he could consume a batch of whodunits which took weeks to get and the writers collectively months to write. And like the princess we had to keep pleasing, if not a capricious emperor, our mystery-devouring professor—in order to get our story.

Soon we looked upon him as our ally. Not only did we expect him to tell us the story of his Shaw association but we thought he might help us get an article from the literary genius whose well-publicized fee was a dollar a word. Fitzgerald remembered reading on our masthead, "*Contempo* does not pay for contributions."

One morning Dr. Henderson was checking our dwindling titles; we cornered him and told him of our extravagant dreams. He nodded vaguely, with his eyes fixed on a book jacket that showed a red dagger sunk in a victim's back. We were impressed. He promised to tell us the story, but warned us that he had no influence with the Prophet of Ayot St. Lawrence. We were delighted when he invited us to Fordell, his mansion on the campus edge. Fordell housed the largest private collection of Shaviana in the world.

As we sat in the cozy, oak-paneled room, much like Ftizgerald's at the Inn, but overflowing with books, magazines, newspapers, and scrapbooks—all in apple-pie order—the professor told us of his dream about Shaw. He had started collecting his work before that historic night in Chicago, 1903, when he saw Shaw's new comedy, *You Never Can Tell*. Convinced of his hero's many-sided talent, he decided to hitch his star to Shaw's. He wrote him a long letter expressing unqualified belief in his genius and asked to become his official biographer.

"It was that simple," Dr. Henderson told us. "Months later I received a postcard from Shaw. It said, 'Send your photograph.' That is all. I was thrilled."

We laughed and the professor went on. "I sent him my photo along with five pages to show my qualifications. I waited. There was no airmail those days. Months later another postcard. It said, 'You'll do.' "

"Couldn't Shaw have sent a çable?" I remember Fitzgerald asking. "It was only two words."

From that day Henderson had Shaw as his daily companion for the rest of his life. During two decades, with Mrs. Henderson as librarian and researcher, he had written millions of words published in eight volumes covering all aspects of the man and his work. Fitzgerald was surprised to hear that the professor had written so much; he had never heard of him.

"He was then editing an expanded and completely rewritten version of his earlier biography of Shaw," I said, pointing to the big volume in my private collection which Fitzgerald had seen. "Perhaps the most comprehensive work by a modern Boswell."

This had been Professor Henderson's documented answer to Frank Harris's recently published "unauthorized" biography of Shaw. Less scurrilous and sensational than Harris's *Confessions of Oscar Wilde*, the book had a vogue on two continents, giving Shaw's friends and enemies a few laughs and snickers. For a time it seemed the rascal Harris had brought the Prophet down to the level of a mortal whose only claim to fame was an extraordinary ego that had crystalized in an overintellectualized body.

We had stumbled on a first-rate controversy—Shaw versus Harris via Henderson. We had asked the professor to answer Harris for his "assembled pseudo-biography" of Shaw. I showed Fitzgerald the Henderson article in *Contempo* and he read it with interest. He seemed delighted with the controversy, and added that he had disliked Harris for his kind of pornography.

The gods were on our side helping to boost *Contempo*. As this article appeared, Harris collapsed and died. We sent condolences to his widow, Nellie, in Nice and mailed copies of the issue to several writers and editors, asking them to defend or further damn Harris in our forthcoming Harris Memorial Number. We received eulogies, comments, blasts from friends and enemies, and from Lord Alfred Douglas, key figure in the Oscar Wilde biography.

Fitzgerald noticed that we had headlined Lord Alfred's letter, "Mass for Harris." He read it with relish. I quote from it: "I have made friends with Shaw after a twenty-year feud, and have several letters from him. Shaw sent me a copy of Harris's biography of himself inscribed as follows: 'To Lord Alfred Douglas another victim of Frank's failings as a biographer from G. Bernard Shaw.' Harris's death removed the last of my enemies. I cannot pretend to feel any regrets at the old ruffian's departure. But I had a Mass said for him in the Catholic Church."

I told Fitzgerald that for an epitaph we had run the last two lines of a page-long poem submitted by a persistent poet. We used it as a "filler." The two lines which brought, not an angry reply, but a grateful note from the poet, were, "You died in time, Frank./You died in time."

Fitzgerald reminded me that I hadn't yet explained how I got that letter from Shaw. I told him that among all the authors to whom we had written for material, in addition to Wolfe, Hemingway, and himself, Shaw was another who had ignored us. At one time or another all of us took a fling at writing Shaw and sending him *Contempo*. It had become a game: who would be the lucky one to hear from him? Henderson's story of how he had succeeded with Shaw spurred me to try the Prophet with one last tug at his beard. I told Fitzgerald this was the gist of the letter:

"Dear G.B.S.: Who the hell do you think you are, not answering us? We've heard from Saint Joan, Methuselah, Antony, Cleopatra, Caesar, Liza Doolittle, and Mrs. Warren. Glance at the *Contempo*s we sent you for their sassy remarks about you. We've wasted thirteen letters asking for a bright gem or a faded fragment. This may be your lean year. In that case I suggest five ideas: What does eating carrots have to do with the color of your beard? Is it true your sex life began at twenty-nine, as that louse Frank Harris claims? What do you think of your Boswell and our neighbor Dr. Archibald Henderson? What about Joyce's singsong dillydallying with your language? Are London fogs really good for Irish wakes?"

Whether it was my letter or the professor's forthcoming book, Shaw replied within a month with a full-page, single-spaced, four-hundred-word letter, with corrections in his own hand. I told Fitzgerald that we had gone dizzy looking at it. Word got around fast. Students flocked in to read it. The bookshop suddenly became a literary mecca.

Henderson was not long in coming to see it. For once he forgot his thrillers. His eyes shone as he read the page, his hands trembled. He gasped, "I must have this letter for my collection!" We were in debt to the Orange Printshop and let him have it for the printing cost of a *Contempo* number. He rushed a photostat to his publisher, D. Appleton and Company; and when the book was published that summer, the letter was reproduced on the back of the jacket.

"Let me see that book again," Fitzgerald said as I reached for it. He took the thousand-page volume from me, turned to the back, and glanced at the letter. He read a bit of it, and I quote the first paragraph:

Professor Henderson's first biography in 1911 did me a signal service. Up to that time I was the victim of half a dozen reputations which seemed to be hopelessly insulated from one another. I was a man who wrote about pictures, a man who wrote about music, a man who wrote about the theatre, a man who wrote novels, a man who wrote plays, a man who wrote about economics, a funny man, a dangerous man, a man who preached at the City Temple, a Shelleyan atheist, a street corner agitator, a leading spirit in the Fabian Society, a vegetarian, a humanitarian, and Heaven knows what else besides; but nobody seemed to know that these men were all the same man. It was Henderson who effected the synthesis. After 1911 the Shaw of the newspapers, though still always fantastic and often absurdly fabulous, got pulled together into a single character. I became an individual where I had not been even a species: I had only been uncollected odds and ends. Henderson collected me, and thereby advanced my standing very materially.

"Sounds as though he wrote you that letter to promote the professor's book about him," Fitzgerald said with a thoughtful smile. "He has more of a knack for exploiting himself than I did."

"I think Shaw called himself a 'publicist,' but the word may have another meaning to the English."

Weeks before the Shaw issue appeared with the letter, Dr. Henderson had gone through our whodunits at least two or three times. Unable to get new ones fast enough, we had slipped him titles he had read earlier. It was simple: he didn't remember them and we kept a card on the titles and dates. It wasn't trickery. We were merely playing his Scheherazade, supplying him with thrillers to keep him happy. The professor read solely for relaxation. More than once the learned man, who taught math and explained Einstein's theory of relativity, made us feel that the jig was up and he was ready for our scalps. Handing me a thriller he had read twice before, he proudly said with a glint in his eye, "I almost figured this one out—about half-way."

Fitzgerald grinned, handed me the heavy book, and reached for my worn copy of Isadora Duncan's *My Life*, saying he would prefer it. He had chosen the book before asking me about Shaw. In fact, it had reminded him to ask about Shaw because of Isadora's legendary letter to him about the kind of child they might produce—and Shaw's unkind reply: "What if it had my beauty and your brains?"

17

Drinking was Fitzgerald's usual method of resting his mind for any period from a couple of hours to several days, although his problems always loomed with urgency when he was sober again. He had another way to distract himself that left no hangover, one that he enjoyed, and yet it didn't give him as much pleasure as drinking. It was inducing others, friends and strangers, to talk about themselves.

For one who usually dominated the conversation, whether with brilliance, maudlin sentiment, or cynical detachment, he maintained a lively and absorbed interest in people that encouraged them to speak freely. In getting others to reveal themselves, Fitzgerald said that he entered into their lives and thoughts, instead of their entering his, and that he identified himself with them and faced the problems of their world. His own problems faded as someone else's took on a personal meaning for him.

His interest in my experiences with Faulkner lay outside that realm, as did his curiosity about Shaw and his Boswell and Thomas Wolfe's mother, a woman he now preferred to forget. But I felt that his questions about other aspects of my life belonged to that special realm. One day we were reminiscing about the various concoctions we had drunk during Prohibition, and I confided to him the key ingredient in that nonalcoholic, eye-catching circus refreshment, pink lemonade, so popular along the sawdust trail during the heyday of the Big Top. It was citric acid.

"It makes a passable gin rickey," Fitzgerald said with a nostalgic smile. "I drank my share. Probably the most wholesome stuff I poured down the hatch in that unsavory era. When I think of the booze we guzzled, a lot of us are lucky to have a few feet of gut left. I bought the best bootleg, yet some of it was raw and tasted like varnish. I don't doubt that it contained wood alcohol."

Fitzgerald said that he had made a list—he was making plenty of lists that summer—of such liquor substitutes as hair tonics, canned heat (Sterno was the brand name), flavoring and baking extracts, that had been sold over the counter. Most could be drunk as they came, but the alcohol had to be distilled from hair tonics and strained out of canned heat. To his list I added three that were popular in the South: Jamaica ginger, Tichnor's antiseptic, and Capudine.

Jamaica ginger had the highest alcoholic content of the flavors and extracts. It was called "jake" and was the best seller in my father's store in Monroe, Louisiana. The recipes on the bottle were for baking, not boozing. We also sold Tichnor's, an antiseptic for cuts and bruises that stung worse on an open wound than Sloan's Liniment. Capudine was a North Carolina favorite, a patent medicine containing a chemical that gave the addicts a doped, jaundiced look.

When mixed with soda pop, either jake or the antiseptic had a solid kick, while Capudine gave a drowsy glow. We dubbed the drinkers of these substitutes, white or black, jakeheads, antheads, and capheads, and we could distinguish one from the other when they entered the store. Jakeheads strode in wide-eyed and loud-mouthed, ready for a fight; antheads shambled in grumbling to themselves, and capheads walked in like zombies and whispered shyly, as if we frowned on their vice.

"You have quite a store of information," Fitzgerald said suspiciously. "You're no rummy—or were you?"

I had drunk rotgut rye, tomato beer, and bathtub gin in college to go along with the gang—so I told him—but my first contact with booze went back to those early years in Louisiana when I watched drunks take a quick one in the rear of our store. They swallowed a little from a pop bottle, refilled it with jake or antiseptic, shook it up, then swigged at the bottle until only foam was left. After belching, they would wipe their mouths on the back of their hands and stagger from behind the feed sacks as though the store were a blind tiger.

Uncle Sam got wise to jake and cracked down on its wide use as a beverage. The manufacturers were ordered to switch from grain alcohol to synthetic alcohol, and they sold the new mixture in bottles labeled "double-strength." Now it was carried only in drugstores and its price was tripled. Jakeheads cursed Uncle Sam but paid the new price, under the illusion that "double-strength" meant it contained a double kick—which in a way it did. A few years later jakeheads were hobbling the streets like derelicts; it was believed that the new formula had damaged the tissues of their knees and ankles.

Those were the Boom days when most consumer products were still the unrestrained blessing of free enterprise, along with Eldorado oil stocks and salted gold mines, and it was up to the buyer to beware; the days in the early twenties when, as a schoolboy, I peddled balloons along the route of circus parades, selling red ones for twice the price of other colors because red was what all the kids wanted; the days when I drove a Model-T at thirty-five miles an hour and was fined for speeding as I delivered the "makings" to bootleggers in the bayous and swamps.

The makings were lawful, but not the making. Loaded down with corn sugar and cane, sacks of rye, bran, corn, cases of fruit jars, rubber hoses, siphons, and heavy brown crocks, the Model-T bounded over the gravel roads and muddy ruts that ended in the bayous. The swamps and bayous were said to be infested with alligators and cottonmouths, cutthroats and outlaws. Gunfire was common enough, the bootleggers taking potshots at revenue officers whose price for playing ball was too high. The scene was appropriate to menace. Gnarled and twisted trees jutted out of gloomy brackish water, tattered gray moss hanging eerily from their naked branches. A silent man picked up the stuff in a canoe, leaving me at the swamp's edge, and rowed back toward the tall grasses where plumes of smoke rose from hidden copper stills.

The Boom days also had moonlit nights when the Ku Klux Klan rode in hooded white robes, burning crosses that were the symbol of white Anglo-Saxon supremacy. Negroes and foreign-born were terrorized into keeping their places as second- and third-class Americans. Six Italians, awaiting trial for robbery and murder in Arkansas, were lynched and their bodies tossed into the Mer Rouge River that flows from razorback Arkansas into hardshell northern Louisiana. A Negro, accused of "sassing" a white woman somewhere in the parish, was strung up, then the body was tied to the back of a truck and doused with kerosene, till it became a flaming torch that was dragged through black quarters as a warning to keep away from Southern white women.

"The bastards," Fitzgerald said, his jaw set tightly. "The bastards."

But when I had told my father about it, he said for me to mind my business. He was a Sicilian immigrant who had made his start in America as a peddler and, with more luck than shrewdness, had become a substantial merchant and importer in Louisiana. Though he was highly thought of in Monroe business circles and we drove a late-model Studebaker Phaeton, this did nothing for my prestige at school, where I was, along with a few other foreign-born, one of the dago boys from the wrong side of the tracks.

Business was business to my father and all of his friends, Italian, Greek, Syrian, or American. His was the booming business of buying and selling. Buying carloads of flour and corn meal, stock feed, sugar, lard, cigarettes, olive oil and cheese, and bootlegger "makings" to sell in our new store on Five Points. Buying property and building houses to rent or sell, in order to buy more land on which to build and then sell. Buy cheap, sell high. But not too high. Keep it moving, turn it over fast, don't let it cool. It was the fever of the twenties, and my father had a bad case of it. Don't worry about money, he would say, there's plenty more where it came from.

I hadn't wanted that money, I told Fitzgerald. I had a different goal. My dream was of having a different sort of life, a sort that couldn't be nourished by the rapacious materialism of everyone around me. My father was blind and deaf to such a notion; my schoolmates were too busy with sports and dances to listen. My mother was long since dead, but a wonderful teacher did listen and gave me advice. And Nick the Greek, who ran the Dixie Lunch, offered me money with which to go to college; then my brother lent me the money that would free me from the store and let me pursue the dream.

But before my brother offered that loan—so I told Fitzgerald—I had run away from the store three times, to "grift" with the circus as an independent operator selling balloons and pink lemonade and spieling for a gypsy "mitt camp," which is the circus name for a palmistry tent. The last time round I was taught the palmist's art by Smaranda, who, as I barked outside her tent, "Knows All, Sees All, Tells All."

"Why didn't you read my hands when I asked you to?" Fitzgerald interrupted. He turned his hands over, palms up, extending them. "You saw something awful? Something you didn't want to tell me?"

"I should've read them the night I met you," I said. "The way your Dollar Woman did mine. What I see now would be hard to separate from what I know about you. It's confusing and bound to influence me."

"Can't you pretend I'm a stranger?"

"I'll try some other time," I hedged.

"It doesn't matter," he said, dropping his hands. "Go on, the gypsy."

I had three circus friends. Two were fortunetellers. Smaranda read hands, while the Old Man with the Flute had a parakeet that picked up cards from a box in its cage. He was a kindly man who had helped me stow away in a gondola car of the circus train, but his method of telling fortunes was to enchant the bird with his music while it chose a card. The old man was a fixture in the circus, driving the torch wagon that led the caravan out of town when the big show was over.

My third friend was Archy the Human Fly, a small fellow no bigger than I. He was an orphan and I had told him I was one too. Often I was with him when he slipped into his red-spangled velvet cape, and I rarely missed his daredevil act inside the Big Top. I never wished him good luck, for among the superstitious circus folk as throughout show business, that would have been bad luck. But with my heart in my mouth as I watched his performance, I sincerely wished it.

It was because of my combined heart and head line in both hands—what Fitzgerald's Dollar Woman had called the Napoleon line—that the gypsy had offered to teach me palmistry. She gave me lessons in the morning while the canvas was going up on the lot, and sometimes in the afternoon when the midway drowsed under a hot sun.

One gloomy afternoon of drumming rain and high wind, the show was almost canceled. The Big Top was only one-third full, the midway was deserted. No spieler's bark rose, no gillies—circus for suckers—tramped outside our flapping tent. I was ready to go and watch Archy put on his cape, but the gypsy took my hands and began to explain the difference in fate lines, holding them as though intent on keeping me at her side.

When the windjammers—the band—waltzed into Archy's music, it was my cue to head for the big tent, and I sprang up.

"Dark weather," the gypsy moaned, her eyes gazing outside the tent. "Evil weather."

Her voice carried a foreboding beyond the nature of the weather, wild as it was. I was suddenly frightened. She lifted her head and stared toward the Big Top as though the canvas walls surrounding us and the big tent had been ripped away by the wind. She stood waiting for something, her eyes rapt, her long black braids hanging like whips. Her silver bracelets that tinkled with the music of little bells were silent.

"Somebody gonna—?" I couldn't say the last word.

"Die?" She pointed at the Big Top. Her emerald ring flashing, she whispered, "Human Fly."

I couldn't move. In my mind's eye I could see the gillies watching Archy climb up the king pole. They would be spellbound and open-mouthed, huddled on the single planks of the bleachers. My spine tingled as it did when I watched his flying leaps. He would be climbing higher and higher, on up into the umbrella cone of ropes and spotlights at the center of the tent, where finally he was shrunk in size to a flyspeck.

The animal-like cries of hundreds of voices rose in the Big Top. Then the hush. The sudden explosion of their shrieks tore me from the spot. I ran toward the half-open flap, but the gypsy grabbed my arm and held me. The crowd was screaming, the windjammers crashed into a rousing march to drown out the panic.

"Don't," she said. "Stake came loose in mud. King pole off balance. His slip broke giant wire."

I wrenched myself from her grip and ran out, zigzagging across the rain-soaked lot, splashing through puddles, stumbling into gillies bursting from the tent. As I entered I saw my friend being carried off on a stretcher under his red-spangled cape. A brawling band of circus clowns dashed into the arena and the cries of spectators switched from distress to bursts of laughter, as if it had only been an act and Archy were still alive.

"I could've killed her."

"Why?" Fitzgerald asked, intent.

"Why?" I repeated. "She knew Archy was doomed. She could've saved him. It was like she had let a blind man walk off a cliff. The last I saw of her, she was standing by the tent flap, looking at me as I ran off the circus grounds."

"You never saw her again?"

"Never."

"Utterly fascinating," he said. "Gypsy fortunetellers fascinate me. Zelda's mother named her after a gypsy queen in a novel she once read. Before I met you, I was writing a story about a gypsy—yes, a fortuneteller. It lacked what you made me feel. Mood and tense atmosphere. It's one of my poorest stories."

"You can't rewrite it?"

He didn't reply.

"Do you think Archy would have listened to your gypsy?"

"Perhaps."

"Never. He would have been through. He never could have scaled that pole again. That would have been a more tragic end for him than crashing in his act." He studied me as though expecting a reply. I was silent. "Your experiences in the twenties are lively and engrossing material. You should use them while you're young—not waste time on the barnyard stuff that ruined Tom Boyd."

"Someday I will."

"Someday," he grimaced. "If you don't bog down in ballyhoo or lose your way along the Party line."

18

When Fitzgerald returned Isadora Duncan's *My Life*, he was in a talkative but disconsolate mood. His depression that afternoon must have drawn on the note of doom sounded in her tragic story. A rash had broken out on his body, and he brooded over it, not doubting that it involved Rosemary or Lottie, or both. In spite of his preoccupation with it, he didn't mention the rash until he had spoken at length about Isadora. Indeed, he was so fascinated by her that I thought he must have read the book before and have borrowed it to refresh his memory.

Passing over her tumultuous love life, Fitzgerald dwelt on the similarities between them that he discovered in her story—their rebellious Irish natures, their being Westerners, their early success and notoriety, and the jagged graph of their flamboyant, unhappy lives in America and on the Riviera. He was struck by the fact that their brilliant careers had moved into eclipse and that they were almost forgotten before reaching forty. Isadora had met a spectacular death in 1927, three months before the publication of her memoirs.

Fitzgerald's biographers record an encounter he had with her two summers earlier. Scott and Zelda were dining with their friends Sara and Gerald Murphy on the promontory-like terrace of an inn overlooking the bay of Isadora's beloved Nice. She sat at a table nearby drinking champagne with three men. She was no longer the lissome dancer of her twenties, but was a striking figure in her purple Grecian robes. The two celebrities had never met.

Fitzgerald now spoke of that occasion. But first he asked me if I had read two articles which he had "fixed up" and sold to his friend Arnold Gingrich of *Esquire*. I said that I had. In one of them, a nostalgic piece on the Scott-and-Zelda heyday, Isadora was described as "too old and fat to care whether people accepted her theories of life and art," and that the champagne in which "she gallantly toasted the world's obliviousness" was "lukewarm."

That summer in 1925, Isadora was forty-six. She may have been fat, but she was still a magnificent-looking woman. (Fitzgerald himself was twenty-nine, Zelda twenty-five; on the basis of his obsession with age, they were a bit old themselves.) There was a touch of malice in those words—Zelda's, not his, he assured me. Fitzgerald said he hadn't written the article, only fixed it up to get quick money to pay her hospital bills. Her ungenerous description was directly connected with what had happened that evening, and her subsequent attempt to become a dancer.

Fitzgerald had risen from their table and had gone to sit at Isadora's feet. He hadn't known the dancer; Gerald Murphy had pointed her out to him. He was given to such theatrical gestures upon meeting famous people. He had earlier sat at Gertrude Stein's feet and, upon meeting James Joyce, Fitzgerald had declared as a mark of his highest esteem that he was going to jump out of the window.

While he sat gazing up at Isadora, who immediately recognized him, she ran her fingers through his fine blond hair and called him her "centurion." That much was known, he said, but not their conversation. What he told me that afternoon I jotted down on the flyleaf of her book. Fitzgerald had said to Isadora that he admired her as "a revolutionary American woman and artist."

"My granny's Irish blood," Isadora said. "She went West as a girl in a covered wagon back in forty-nine. She taught me Irish jigs and inspired me as a child."

"I am Gaelic too."

"I could tell from your writing. You're our dancing writer, just as Nietzsche is our dancing philosopher."

He accepted the tribute modestly; even in telling about it he inclined his head. Isadora spoke of having been asked to write her memoirs and of having agreed for the money. Now the advance was spent, time had passed, and the publisher was pressing her to deliver the manuscript she hadn't yet written.

"I'm struggling with it. I'm a dancer, I know nothing about writing. The truth frightens me, but I must tell it."

"The truth or nothing."

"Yes, truth is nobler than pride."

Isadora asked if he would help her. He agreed with the gallant feeling of saving a lady in distress. By his account, she was a magnetic woman. As she rose to leave with her companions, Isadora took Fitzgerald by the hand and told him the name of her hotel in a voice that undoubtedly reached his table. Fitzgerald had heard that Isadora sometimes chose a lover for the night in this fashion, but he felt that her interest in him was due to her needing help with her book.

The story has often been told of what Zelda did at the time, yet I must retell it here—out of its proper order, since Fitzgerald did not mention it until later. According to the story, it was Zelda who now had the impulse to jump, but not out of a window. She climbed on her chair and flung herself across the table down a short flight of stone steps. An iron gate at the foot of the steps saved her from a fall that might have killed her. The Murphys, stunned by her self-destructive act, rushed after her and found that while she was cut and bruised, she wasn't seriously hurt. Without a word Zelda went into the inn to restore her appearance. Fitzgerald never saw Isadora again.

That afternoon in my bookshop he wondered—without mentioning Zelda's fugue—whether Isadora had indeed invited him to be her lover. Might he be a type to attract her? He was taken by the idea. To judge from her book, it seemed to him that her lovers tended to be more aesthetic and sensitive than was consistent with the American ideal of that period. He too had to be aesthetic and sensitive because of his profession, even though he struggled unsuccessfully to achieve the rugged façade of American manliness. He hadn't ever outgrown the conventional image of feminine desirability: a fragile, girlish prettiness. No, he wouldn't have been comfortable as Isadora's lover. She was too overpowering a woman and, like himself, she seemed to need love-making for her own art. On the other hand, he admitted that she had attracted him by her sheer vitality.

I thought to myself, then and later, that Fitzgerald unconsciously sought dominant women, but at the same time found himself resisting their domination. If the woman also embodied his ideal of the American beauty, apparently he didn't, in his personal life, probe deeply beneath the surface. His eye was surer in his novels. "Strength," "cowardice," "weakness" were words that he often used in our conversations; they represented concepts that still stood squarely in the twenties and thirties. Zelda, the most beautiful, feminine, yet dominant woman he had known, was the embodiment of all his conflicting ideals.

He went on talking about Isadora as though he had drunk champagne with her the night before. He was fascinated by her extraordinary life, and from time to time would pick up her book and comment on some passage. A remarkable woman he observed, self-educated and highly developed in her character through the combination of great talent, capacity for joy, and the terrible, unexpected blows of life. With little schooling, she had appreciated Dickens, Thackeray, Shakespeare, and pursued an understanding of Plato, Kant, Nietzsche, Marx, and Darwin, to many of whom he was also indebted for his own outlook.

Another aspect of her life style with which Fitzgerald identified strongly was that expressed in certain desperate modes of conduct. He traced its source to the poetic recognition that life is essentially tragic. Dressed in a tunic, Duncan would dance the night through to Beethoven, Wagner, and Chopin played by a pianist in her entourage, while champagne flowed in her villa filled with the celebrities and the fashionable rich of the day. Her pleasure-seeking adventures on the Riviera—the yachts, sports cars, all-night fêtes—helped to inspire the extravagant and reckless style of Fitzgerald's own generation.

She had psychic powers, too, having premonitions, prophetic dreams, and visions throughout her life. She consulted readers of cards, hands, stars, and kept a personal fortuneteller in her household, in quest of revelations that would protect and guide her. Fitzgerald believed that her interest in the occult had replaced her cast-off religion. At one time she had thought herself going mad and had been haunted by the image of Nijinsky in his asylum. With the loss of her two children, foretold in a vision of death, her dance interpretations were given over to the spirit of tragedy. Fitzgerald was visibly affected as he spoke of this. Tragedy was linked to the dance for him, too; Zelda's attempt to become a dancer had brought about her breakdown.

"I believe that although one may seem to go on living, there are some sorrows that kill."

These were Isadora's words, written some years after the death in a motor accident of her two children, Deirdre and Patrick, on the road to Versailles. Fitzgerald opened the book and showed the passage to me. It was underlined in pencil, which it hadn't been before. I remembered that he had marked my copy of *Taps at Reveille*.

He riffled the pages of her book and stopped to glance at another passage. Then he turned to me and unexpectedly asked if I had seen Lottie. I went to the card file and found that she hadn't been in for two weeks. Hesitating, but with a show of calmness, Fitzgerald told me about the rash that was spreading on his back and legs.

"Do you think I could have caught something from her, even with her negative report?"

"Why don't you see a doctor about a test?"

"I can't do it here," he said flatly. "I don't want anybody to know."

"I'm not going to tell anybody."

"Christ, it would have to happen to me!"

"But you don't know. There's no need to worry."

"I feel tainted. I won't take all that mercury," he said. "I've been thinking of Rosemary. What if she gave it to her husband—after I gave it to her. What a hell of a present!"

"How long have you had it?"

"Over a week—only a spot or two at first."

"Ever had this before?"

"I can't think of anything more horrible and revolting than syphilis," he said, paying no attention to me. "I've been lucky. And careful. I'll never take another chance with her kind—if I know it."

"What makes you think it was Lottie?"

"It couldn't be Rosemary." He thought a moment. "Though I did go to New York and there was—"

He suddenly changed the subject and told me he was still hearing from Rosemary. A note of bitterness had crept into her letters. She asked him if he had forgotten her and if he had another girl to keep him company on his sleepless nights.

"The poor, dear, lovely girl. I once told her that relationships had an unfortunate way of wearing out like everything else," he said sadly. "She's so afraid I will forget her. The hell of it is that I think I still love her. She hangs on to the hope that we will be back together again. Christ!"

Fitzgerald slammed the Duncan book on the desk and walked out of the shop without another word. I picked up the green-backed volume to place it on the shelf. It fell open at a page with another marked line: "Hope is a hard plant to kill and no matter how many branches are knocked off and destroyed, it will always put forth new shoots."

19

A day or so after Fitzgerald asked about Lottie, she appeared with her poodles at the symphony office. It was the first time I had seen her dressed in gray. That early afternoon her hair wasn't perfectly groomed, and her usual gaiety and insouciance were missing. Sitting with her in the Arcade Coffee Shop a few minutes later, I noticed that she was tense as well as tired and preoccupied. I could only speculate on whether her loss of vivacity and good looks was due to her two- or three-week jaunt or to the night she had just spent with Fitzgerald.

As we entered the coffee shop a haughty-faced hostess tried to stop us at the door. No dogs were allowed. Lottie put on as haughty a face and announced to the air that her poodles were people. Flicking the leashes for the dogs to precede her, she marched in grandly. The hostess retreated, although she was still grumbling about Lottie to the cashier when I paid the check. We sat in a far corner, the dogs curled under the table at her feet. Having won her point, Lottie wanted no further word on that score. She was filled with concern, annoyance, and indignation—but over Fitzgerald.

"I thought your friend was cute at first. He still is, in a way, like a spoiled, naïve kid," she said after ordering coffee. "He called while I was at the Château. It was urgent life-and-death stuff. I had to see him. I canceled a date and went to the Inn. And you know what it was? Don't try—you can't guess. It reminds me of the time he asked me, without batting an eye, to show him a clean bill of health."

She glanced around the quiet café—it was after the noon rush—and lowered her voice. Fitzgerald's purpose in seeing her was to ask her if she had any connection with a rash on his body. I didn't betray that I knew anything about it. The idea, she said, that he would think such a thing! Her voice again rose for a moment. It was an insult to her profession, her good health, and all the solid citizens she had been accommodating since the Crash.

"Well, he apologized, but he took off his shirt to show me this thing breaking out on his chest and back. The fool started scratching it. I warned him to stop or he'd spread it. Then he pulled up a trouser leg to show me where it was on his shin. I said it didn't look like a symptom of what he was afraid of, but that he ought to see a doctor instead of worrying about it and accusing innocent women. He finally agreed. He made me a drink and sat down near me on the couch. I guess he was surprised I didn't shy away from him. He asked me if I didn't think it was contagious. What I don't know, I said, never bothers me. He'd never take such a chance if *I* had that rash. Anyhow, I made myself comfortable."

She told me that she had put her legs on the couch and let her pumps fall to the floor. Fitzgerald took her feet in his hands and admired them. They were trim and well shaped, he said, like a dancer's. Lottie remarked that she hadn't danced with anybody she liked in years. He caressed her feet, the toes, instep, and heel, and got an odd pleasure out of it. He spoke all the while in a soft, soothing voice, saying she should have gone on the stage.

What he was doing to her had a calming effect on her body and spirit, she said, and before she knew it, Lottie was telling him of her struggle to become an actress. She spoke of her family's objection, that the stage was the road to sin; of being stranded with a road company at the time of the Crash, and having to get back to New York the best way she could. It was then that she decided to try another profession—other actresses were doing it—because she couldn't see herself settling down as "one man's squaw."

I wondered whether the story was true or she had dreamed it up on the spot to flatter Fitzgerald on his insight. There was the ring of sincerity in her voice and, as I had told him, she had never lied to me. Other than that, it occurred to me that I knew very little about her.

"He proposed that if I liked him, I should dance with him to break the bad luck in my partners. Then he pulled off my silk stockings so I wouldn't get a run. He was very sweet the way he peeled them off. When he finished he got up, offered me his hand in a gallant way, and whirled me around the room in a slow waltz. There wasn't any music, but it was playing, I guess, in his head because he didn't miss a beat.

"After a few more turns he stopped, saying he hoped I meant what I said about his rash not bothering me because . . ." She hesitated, taking a deep breath, and then shrugged. "Hell, he's your friend. He wanted me right then and there. He simply had to have me. It seems that the sight of women's feet has excited him since he first started thinking about sex.

"It was then and there, right on the couch. I remember him telling me he only made love to help him write. No wonder he was so quick. He might know how to write but he sure doesn't know about this other thing. And he gave me no chance to tell him to take his time, breathe deeply, or think of something else. When it was all over and I mentioned it to him, he started bawling like a sot. I can't stand crying drunks. But I felt sorry for him. Because of what he told me about his loony wife.

"Listen to this." Then she paused. "Years ago she told him he could never satisfy her or any other woman because he was built so small. Can you beat that? It really hit him hard. And he believed her because he thought she was smart, and because he knew little about it himself. Then he told me, he'd never had a woman till he fell in love with her.

"He kept crying and talking. What he wanted to know from me, since I had been with many men, was if his wife was right about this. I felt like laughing, but I didn't. So I told him he was like all the men I knew and he ought to forget what she had said. But he didn't believe I was telling him the truth. I then told him that making a woman happy was more a matter of pleasing her—of technique—than the size of a certain thing. This loving way came natural to some men, but experience helped, and no two women were pleased in the same way. That's why I promised to give him a few tips to pleasure them and to control himself. He wanted them then and there. I told him a couple, but there's no need to draw you a picture. . . ."

Fitzgerald still wanted to be reassured that she was leveling with him about being like other men. He also asked her to keep seeing him. She said she would and started to leave. He appeared to have calmed down and was ready for sleep, until she reached the door, and he rose to stop her. Looking at her with his tearful, bloodshot eyes, he asked her why his wife would say such a thing if it weren't true.

She was unbalanced, Lottie told him. He argued that Zelda wasn't ill at the time and ought to have known what she was talking about. His fixation annoyed Lottie. She bluntly told him that his wife was not only mad but didn't know as much about men as *he* thought she did. Fitzgerald clutched her hand, repeating with alcoholic persistence, "Then *why* did she say it?"

"I told him I'd think about it and let him know when he was sober.

He said I didn't have to think about it and he was sober now and I had to tell him. I couldn't hold back what I'd been thinking from the moment he told me what she'd said. So I told him his wife had to be nuts to think what she did and a bitch to say it, and that he was a naïve, damn fool to believe it all these years. He called me a whore and slapped me. The first time a man had done that—except my father. I walked out. He was sobbing and begging me to come back."

Then Lottie was silent. She had spoken with more emotion than I had seen her display in all the time I had known her.

"Lottie, I'm sorry I got you into this."

"It's not your fault." She picked up her shoulder bag, ready to leave. "He's cost me plenty, but that doesn't matter. He's got me worrying about him. Something I haven't done over a man in years. He needs somebody. Do you know his wife?"

"No. She's in Johns Hopkins in Baltimore. He's thinking of bringing her here next year."

"The poor sweet idiot," Lottie said in an affectionate tone. Now she was noticeably more relaxed. We rose to go. She held the dogs' leashes firmly. Then she said, "Daisy was merciful. She helped to kill Gatsby. What did his crazy wife want to do—cripple him for life?"

A few days later I saw Fitzgerald. He didn't mention Lottie, but his thoughts were taken up with the rash. He had decided to have a Wasserman made under an assumed name, but he was anxious nevertheless to have my opinion on it. My protest of complete ignorance about skin eruptions didn't prevent him from taking me down to the men's room in the hotel. He took off his jacket, tie and shirt, so as to show me the ugly spots on his body.

A Negro attendant stepped over to offer us soap and a towel. Fitzgerald fixed on him with interest and asked if he thought the condition meant he had caught something. The white-haired, solemn-faced black studied it a moment, and shook his head. He thought that Fitzgerald might have eaten or drunk something that didn't agree with him.

"Like what?"

"Strawberries and suchlike." He noticed Fitzgerald wavering as he leaned near a urinal. "Could be that fancy new likker. Ain't good as it was before Prohibition. But it cost a heap more and I hear makes some folks sick."

"Maybe you're right, grandpa. Thanks," Fitzgerald said. He dug in his pocket and handed the attendant a dollar bill, gesturing for him to keep the change.

"Thank you, sir. I hope it ain't serious."

The Negro retired to the outer alcove. I went to a urinal. Fitzgerald, at the one beside me, glanced over.

"You Latins!" he said in a playful envious tone.

"Oh?" I remembered with a jolt what Lottie had told me. Moving away, I returned the inquisitive glance, and said, "You Celts!"

"Don't you think it's a bit . . . ?"

"Hell no," I said, forcing a latrine-talk assurance. "I've seen some like my thumb."

"That's pretty short."

"It can still do the job."

"Some women are hard to please." He flushed the water and went over to the washstand.

"Yes, a few are frigid," I said, trying to sound casual, but feeling my way carefully. I didn't want to say anything that might betray Lottie's confidence. "But a lot more men are clumsy lovers. Fortunately, most women don't know it yet."

"Think so?" he asked with a dubious look. "Or they're only being kind."

"What about Rosemary?"

"She was madly in love with me."

"That can make all the difference—according to Van de Velde and a lot of others."

"Who's Van de Velde?"

I told him about his book *Ideal Marriage*, which Fitzgerald was to borrow and in which I later made notes on this episode. Fitzgerald said he was leaving the next day for Charlotte or Spartanburg for the test. If the result was positive, he would wire Rosemary so that she and Ogden could do something about it. As for himself, he was going to dive off a dock or a boat somewhere. This would make it appear that his death was accidental, and Zelda and Scottie could collect his life insurance.

When we walked out of the hotel and strolled toward Grove Arcade, I noticed Lottie walking her poodles in front of the new post-office building. Fitzgerald pretended he didn't see her. He again took up the thread of our men's-room discussion.

"Ernest and I once talked about the same thing. He said I was all right too. I didn't believe him then. I was having my problems with Zelda. Probably I wouldn't believe him because he thought Zelda was crazy. Now that she's hopeless, he was right about her, and probably about this other thing too."

Except for Lottie, I wouldn't have known the nature of this problem between him and Zelda. Nor did he tell me what Hemingway said about Zelda's charge; I had to wait decades to find out in *A Moveable Feast*. When Fitzgerald asked him why Zelda would say there was "something wrong" with him, Hemingway had replied, "To put you out of business. That's the oldest way of putting people out of business."

Though Lottie and Hemingway had used different words, the substance was remarkably similar, and I prefer hers: "What did his crazy wife want to do—cripple him for life?"

20

Fitzgerald went out of the state for the test. I saw him the afternoon he came downtown to telephone the doctor's office for the report. Anxious to remain incognito, he wouldn't call from the Inn. He received the news with a sense of defeat, as though his worst fears had been confirmed. I had seen that look before during the summer and did not jump to conclusions; still, remembering his talk of drowning himself if the test turned out positive, I was concerned about him.

"The report was negative, wasn't it?" I asked hopefully.

He nodded but said nothing for a bit.

"That makes it worse. I was all keyed up for action, not sticking around. It means I'll have to face the whole damn mess all over again." He began pacing the floor of the bookshop as he spoke, Hamlet to the life, weary and intense, and I thought it was a good performance. "A new life must begin for me out of this stinking wreckage, or it's down the drain. I've made these resolves before and disappointed some of my oldest friends. I can't go on drifting, wasting emotion and talent.

"There's no ducking it. We all have a fatal flaw. I know mine, and I'm meant to resolve it myself. That is my fate. Someone said it was in my hand. Probably my Dollar Woman." He held up a hand and looked at his palm. "If that's it, I have two choices. There are always two choices and they're often both lousy. I'll either pull out of this or go under. No half way this time. I must find a way back, as a writer, or head straight for the nearest exit and say good-by. I know my duty—to myself and those close to me. But I can't go at it blindly. I have to follow my fate with my eyes wide open."

Suddenly he glanced with disgust at his slightly protruding belly. He slapped it a couple of times and cursed himself.

"God, I'm swelling up like a beer barrel. There has to be a change. A drastic change."

His restlessness had brought him several times to my desk, where he fingered a book as he spoke. Some issues of *Contempo* lay there. He picked one up and said that its type face was the same as that in which Scribners set his books. He went on to say that he had asked Max Perkins to keep his books uniform in dark-green cloth binding, gold lettering, and other typographical details.

From my collection I took down the copy of *Taps at Reveille* that he had autographed and looked at a page. It was Caslon, like *Contempo*, and in the same type size, too. I set the book and magazine side by side for us to examine. This coincidence seemed to give him a friendlier feeling toward *Contempo* and set it apart from his general condemnation of avant-garde publications as "cuckoo magazines."

He was curious to know the role played by Gorham Munson, the critic, in relation to *Contempo*. Munson's name was on the masthead along those of Dos Passos, Anderson, Dreiser, Joyce, Lewis, Pound, Cowley, Mumford, Caldwell, and others. I replied that Munson had helped to direct our policy more toward newer and experimental writers than toward established ones.

"You were lucky to have such a man to guide you," Fitzgerald said. "When *The Bookman* was still alive, Munson wrote an article for it, I'd say about 1932, on the postwar novel and novelists. He said I was the only important writer in the twenties whose novels weren't botched by naturalism and that if the younger writers had followed my lead the direction of the postwar novel might have been toward poetic fiction. It didn't go that way, of course"—he shrugged—"I was silent for too long after *Gatsby*, and then Ernest's vogue succeeded mine."

While he spoke I opened *Taps at Reveille* at page 384, where Fitzgerald had made a notation the night we met. I had discovered it later and wanted him to explain it. He had crossed out a description of Paris at twilight in the story "Babylon Revisited" and written in the margin, "Used in *Tender*." When I showed it to him, he made an annoyed gesture. The proofreader had made a mistake. Fitzgerald had deleted this paragraph in the final proofs of the book, after carefully rewriting it and marking the revision for insertion in its place.

"But some bonehead put in the rewrite without killing that paragraph," he explained. "So you have them both, one after the other. The first was something I had used with slight variation in *Tender*."

He took the book and turned the pages.

"I asked Max to make sure it would be corrected in future printings—if there were any. But it will probably stay as it is. Here's another boner that nobody caught, and I didn't notice until it was too late."

(He was right about future printings of "Babylon Revisited." I recently checked the last printing and nothing had been done about deleting that paragraph.)

Fitzgerald pointed to a page in "A Nice Quiet Place," in which the heroine, Josephine, is called Rosemary. This happened, he explained, because he was working on *Tender* at the same time and had blindly put down the wrong name. He turned once more to "Babylon Revisited" and showed me another sentence that he had used almost verbatim in the novel. Probably there were other boners, he said; he had been under a cloud of despair at the time, and didn't remember what he had taken out of the novel and what he had left in it.

"Call it self-plagiarism, which isn't as bad as plagiarizing one's contemporaries," he said. "Someday a professor is going to write an article about these mistakes and some heavyweight critic will praise him for his diligent research. After *Paradise* was published, I said that an author ought to write for the youth of his own time, the critics of the next, and the schoolmasters of later years. I was twenty-four and in the limelight. Showing off before my betters was irresistible."

While he was there that afternoon, I had an unexpected visit from Louis Adamic, author of the best-seller *A Native's Return* and one of *Contempo's* first contributing editors. The tall, nervous, slightly stuttering Yugoslav-born writer echoed Fitzgerald's admiration for Mencken, who had printed their first work. Then Adamic announced that he had come South to have a look at Black Mountain College.

Fitzgerald remembered that my friend Bill Buttrick had spoken of the college. Before meeting Bill, I had written a news story on Black Mountain's experimental and community-life approach to education. I had heard of it from William Wunsch, a North Carolinian, who had been Wolfe's early roommate at Chapel Hill. (Wunsch was my botany teacher at the Monroe City High School in the early twenties.) From Louisiana he had gone to Florida, where he was drama coach at Rollins College, perhaps the first such experimental college in the South.

When Professor John A. Rice left Rollins in the heat of a dispute over policy, Wunsch resigned and joined him in planning the new venture at Black Mountain in 1933. It was Wunsch who suggested the site, which was used in summer by the Blue Ridge Assembly of the Protestant Church. Centered around a group of buildings was white-columned Robert E. Lee Hall, with its huge lobby and a sweeping view of the valley and the mountain peaks. It was the place where the Southern Writers Conference was to be held that summer.

Adamic told us that he had been sent by his friend Henry Allen Moe, secretary of the Guggenheim Foundation, who was also a friend of Professor Rice and Black Mountain College. He was to do an article for *Harper's* on the college's advanced ideas of stressing community life and individual creativity, and on its staff, particularly Josef Albers of the Bauhaus Institute, leading exponent of modern functional design. Hitler had closed the Bauhaus in 1933 and driven most of its artists and architects—Albers, Klee, Gropius, Feininger, Kandin.'y, et cetera—out of Germany.

Fitzgerald wanted to know about Black Mountain as a possible college for his daughter, in the event that he moved Zelda to Asheville. But he said that Scottie would need a planned curriculum and a more disciplined setup if she were to get something out of college. (Though he brought Zelda to Highland Hospital the following year, Scottie eventually went to Vassar.) Still, he was intrigued by Black Mountain, particularly since one was free to pursue one's own creative interests there without being hampered by too many community obligations.

(Although Black Mountain shut down in 1956, it proved to be a forerunner of much that is now regarded as modern in the arts, education, and way of life. It is credited with having helped to shape such diverse talents as those of Eric Bentley, John Cage, Merce Cunningham, Buckminster Fuller, Paul Goodman, Franz Kline, Willem de Kooning, and Robert Rauschenberg, all of whom were in residence there either as students or as members of the staff.)

After Fitzgerald left us to meet his secretary and get some work done, Adamic said that he was surprised to find him in such a sober condition.

"He's on the wagon," I said. "No hard stuff. Only beer."

"He looks fine," Adamic said. "I heard he was here for the cure because he'd been drinking himself blind."

"I've only seen him on a bat or two."

"Have you seen much of him?"

"Off and on, most of the summer."

"Then I don't feel bad about my other little mission. When a friend at Scribners heard I was coming down here, he asked me to look him up and report how I found him. I'll tell the friend to stop worrying."

———— 21

For the second time that year Fitzgerald had to face the prospect that no big scene would take place to rescue him from his hopeless state. There was no course left but to go on living and writing so that he might educate Scottie and take care of Zelda. This was his fate; he said he was being driven by fear, duty, and necessity as by a three-pronged whip.

Armed with the best of resolves, he went North to check with Zelda's doctors in Baltimore and go on to New York to see a friend or two and perhaps his daughter. After conferring with the psychiatrists, he started for New York, but he hopped out of the train at a way station and took the next one back to Baltimore. There he picked up gin, went to his usual hotel, and drank himself into an alcoholic stupor that left him, after three days, with a fever and in a pool of sweat.

What the doctors had told him about Zelda may have set him off, although I had feared that he might do something of the sort after his disappointment over the test. He usually needed a reason to trigger such a bust; the disappointment was enough to do it. By this time I had observed that before Fitzgerald could be serious about such a resolve he first had to hit bottom, wallow in disgust and self-pity, atone and repent, and then use that position as a starting point for one of his determined uphill climbs.

Shortly after he returned to Grove Park Inn, he called me one morning to come see him. I found him in pajamas and an old dressing gown he often wore while working. There were papers on the table and the couch; he reached for a pencil behind his ear while mulling over the rough page of a story. There were circles under his eyes, his face was pallid, his beer belly protruded. When he put down the page, I noticed that his hands hardly shook.

"That rash was a kind of eczema," he said, breaking the silence.

"Probably due to the combination of sleeping pills I was taking. The itching stopped as soon as I switched them."

"So it was sleeping pills," I repeated.

"Who knows?" He shrugged, poured a glass of beer, and held it before me. "Too early?"

"Yes, thanks."

"Ten a day is my new regime. So far so good." He cleared a chair and the couch for us to sit, and lit a cigarette. "Before I left I was consuming thirty-five. Yes, a day. The bellboy counted them. That explains this barrel gut. But I'll get it down. Have you seen Lottie?"

"Yesterday," I said and sat in the chair. "She asked for you."

"I owe her an apology. If you see her before I do, please apologize for me. Say it was noninfectious leprosy and that it mystified a dozen Johns Hopkins top brains." He looked at me sideways and without the hint of a smile. "Zelda had the worst kind of eczema after her first break in Paris. The doctors couldn't decide who or what caused it— Scottie, me, her diet, some chemical, or her anxiety over losing precious time.

"Someone got the bright idea that it was psychological. There was a story about a woman who broke out with it when she caught her husband stealing from the baby's piggy bank. I must have done something worse in her eyes, or Scottie. It was a living hell for her. Zelda wished she were dead. They tried everything on her, even hypnosis, but the best cure was for me to stay away from her.

"I had a hell of my own those lonely, sleepless nights in Switzerland. It's the last stop—where nothing begins, but everything ends. I tried to figure out what I had said or done to hurt her that she should have such a violent reaction to me. That was about the time my insomnia began. I tried different combinations of pills, pink, yellow, blue, to get some sleep and rest my nervous system."

I remember the visit as one of his most relaxed. He spoke in a low voice and his manner was contrite, like that of a boy who had been reprimanded for misconduct. It was no grandstand show reminiscent of the interview; he was calm, subdued, introspective. Though his eyes seemed directed inward rather than being focused on me, he wasn't distant or impersonal but warm and confidential.

"It was probably all my fault," he said as if carrying on a conversation with himself. "I shouldn't have taunted her. I can be a bastard when it comes to taunting and accusing people. She had talent. I hated to see it go to waste. She had been too much of a playgirl and there was a lazy or indolent streak in her. That comes naturally to those bred in the sluggish atmosphere of the Deep South. I kept after her, probably in self-defense, to paint or write—even ballet at first— so I could work and so she wouldn't be bored or restless, itching for a dance or a party that often ended at dawn and left us with a hangover that shot the next day for me."

Zelda had once told him that she hoped never to become ambitious about anything. Still, he encouraged her to work, recognizing her flair for clever and descriptive writing. She had written articles for popular magazines, some signed by herself and others that shared his byline— even if she had done all the writing—so they would command his usual high price. And then came her more or less autobiographical novel, *Save Me the Waltz*, at the time of her second breakdown.

Fitzgerald was pouring himself another beer when the buzzer sounded. I went over to open the door; a bellboy was there with a paper carton of beer bottles. Fitzgerald joined us and told me it was his quota for the day. The Negro took them into the other room; before he left he had Fitzgerald initial a room-service check he hadn't signed that morning. Fitzgerald lit another cigarette, sat down opposite me, and went on as though there had been no interruption.

"I was relieved not to see a copy of *Waltz* in your shop. But you have read it."

"Yes," I said and sat down again.

He then told me that Zelda had started the novel in Montgomery and finished it in the Baltimore clinic—"in six obsessive weeks as if driven by the demons that possessed her. It had the material of a classic tragedy, but she couldn't see it any more than she was capable, as a person, of facing it. *Waltz* sprang from the depths of her misery— the wasteland of her shattered ego. I told Perkins it was good and to publish it—to give her a boost. But it remains a bad novel—worse than *Paradise*. What did you think of it?"

I said, "At first I was annoyed by her bizarre style, the strange metaphors, and all those adjectives. I thought it was smart and superficial. Then I was hypnotized by its incantation and its mad vitality. But while reading it I had the odd sensation that the novel had been badly translated from another language."

Fitzgerald appeared to be both annoyed and impressed by my remarks. "Did you review it?"

"Scribners didn't send me a copy."

"I wish you had. Zelda would have liked most of what you said. Yes, it sounded as if it were badly translated from another language. The language of the deep unconscious. Jung's fantastic world. The book was a literary feat of what psychiatrists call 'free association' and Joyce called 'the stream of consciousness.' But it's still a bad novel."

I was silent. After a pause he went on: "The original draft was a hodgepodge that would have embarrassed us both as writers. I revised some passages to give the book form. I did nothing to her prose. I couldn't tamper with her style any more than I could change her after all those years. It was hopeless."

Then he rose, went to refill his glass, and was silent.

"Did you make drastic cuts?" I ventured.

I shouldn't have asked that question. It was stupid of me, the sort of thing one sometimes does to keep the conversation alive. Fitzgerald came out of himself and peered at me with sudden suspicion, as if I had turned up a painful and long-forgotten secret.

"What have you heard?"

"Nothing," I said with an uncomfortable feeling.

"Nothing?"

He looked at me as if I had suddenly become an enemy. A gulf seemed to open between us. I rose and walked away from him.

"You must have heard something—to ask such a question."

"Yes. That the hero was a painter with no talent or personality," I said matter-of-factly without meeting his curious stare. "He was named Amory Blaine. You changed it to David Knight."

"That's true," he said in a cordial tone. "But you asked about drastic cuts. What did you mean?"

I now felt free to speak out and said, "Her attack on you as a writer and a husband."

"What else?"

"Your private life, marriage, quarrels."

"How did you find out?" His voice again was insistent, challenging. "How?"

"I don't remember."

"That's no answer and you know it."

I gazed at the ceiling, neither shaken nor intimidated.

"Who told you?" he asked sharply. "Who?"

"I can't tell you," I said, backing toward the window. "It was told to me in confidence."

"Do I know the person?"

"Probably, I can't say."

"Have you told anyone?"

"Of course not," I said, facing him.

"You expect me to believe you?" he asked, but not as sharply as before.

"Scott," it was one of the few times that I addressed him by his first name, "that's up to you."

I had only to reveal the name of my informant at Scribners' promotion department and all would have been as before with us. During my few years as a reporter I had been taught never to betray a confidence. Fitzgerald went for another bottle, returned with a full glass, and lit a cigarette. I no longer felt uneasy, I was restless; I glanced at my watch, hoping to announce I was due at the Bookshop. But I couldn't leave in such an atmosphere of estrangement.

Fitzgerald calmly sat down and resumed the subject of Zelda's novel, saying that the critics had been unkind, despite everything he had done to improve it. Its sale had been about a thousand copies, and Zelda had received nothing in royalties after the small advance. I sat down again opposite him and asked how she had taken its failure.

"Zelda was a saint about it. The minute we were through with the galleys, she put it behind her and started writing something else."

"Would you say writing it was a kind of therapy?" I hoped that such a question might bring us back to our old intimacy.

"I think so," he said. "I believe Jung said the arts, as mediums of creative expression, can serve as the best outlet for our deepest neuroses. You know Jung?"

"Some, and Freud too. But I prefer Jung."

"So do I," he said in a friendlier tone. "He stresses the unconscious and the creative process, Freud the sexual side of human activity. Writing *Waltz* seemed to have calmed some of her egomania and freed her from competitive drives."

He went on speaking of the book. "It's a bad novel, not a bad book. A psychiatric document of the schizophrenic mind in action. A mind gone berserk, evidently not with a natural drive or ambition, but consumed by a passion to dazzle and show off. I know her better than I know myself. We could be twins. She pushed herself beyond the limit, hoping to blaze a trail as I did. I made it, she broke down."

The phone rang. It was the operator saying that a bellboy was bringing up a package. He thanked her, hung up, and muttered to me, "Rosemary."

I glanced at my watch and said I had to go. He motioned me to stay; I stopped near the door, undecided.

"My apologies for sounding like a movie district attorney. I was surprised you knew so much about me. I guess we were bound to meet, but probably not to be friends. Don't go. Not yet." His voice was more friendly. He picked up the telephone. "Let me order you some lunch."

It was a friendly lunch. We both made an effort to recapture some of the old intimacy, but his reserve lingered. The reserve seemed to be a result more of his sober and penitent mood than of the gap that had begun to open between us. Conversation gave way to revelations in which he aired further disturbing thoughts about Zelda. While saying that he had been responsible for bringing on her destructive malady, Fitzgerald tried to justify the role he had played and to lighten the burden of his guilt about it.

"We lost everything, Zelda and I. Peace, love, and health. Money too, but that was the least of it. I could always dash off a *Post* story or two when we were broke and the weather was right. Peace went first—with our gay and reckless times. Love next—with our quarrels and loss of trust and confidence. Then health—with her demon of insanity and mine of drink that made us mindless enemies.

"Yet we had some of our most beautiful times together after her first break. It was an idyll of recaptured closeness, despite the anxiety of living on the edge of different worlds. Then came her second, to snatch it all from us as if it had been a mirage. And finally the third, to smash all hope of recovery or a change that would make it possible for me to write or sleep again."

He put a hand to his face. I was silent. Then he spoke again: "Did you ever slap your wife?"

"No."

"Probably you didn't have to be a bully." He paused. "She ever call you a fairy or a yellow bastard?"

"Not yet."

"How long have you been married?"

"Three years."

"There's still time or—she's not the type." Another pause. "She doesn't seem jealous of what you want to do."

He was silent again. I remember his pauses, his not looking at me, and his need to unburden himself about Zelda. He sat deep in the couch, not rising for cigarettes or more beer. He seemed to be scanning inner horizons.

"When Zelda said she hoped never to become ambitious, I should have listened, not driven her, thinking it was merely indolence. What she feared, I believe, wasn't ambition so much as the fact that it would possess her. She would have to give herself to it exclusively. Once it possessed her, there would be no rest until she had conquered it or it had destroyed her."

When she decided to study ballet Fitzgerald thought it was impossible at her age, but he didn't object. It was when she plunged into ballet with the frantic determination to become a Pavlova—twenty years too late—that he turned against it. He warned her that it was one of the most difficult of the arts; it called for hours of practice, dedication, and a youthful and flexible body. And though she had been praised as an amateur dancer, he said that there was a wide gap between the amateur and the professional in all the arts.

"I shouldn't have told her that she didn't have the body or was starting too late," Fitzgerald said, nodding to himself. "It was a challenge to start at twenty-seven, and she accepted it. Having no time to lose, she naturally expected quick success. It was like writing *Waltz* in six weeks, which came later. That fall she went into ballet with the frenzy of a ritual dancer invoking the gods. She would be a Pavlova or—"

They were living at the time in an old mansion along the Delaware near Wilmington. She commuted three times a week to Philadelphia to study with Catherine Littlefield, head of the Philadelphia Opera ballet corps. Scottie was six at the time, and she went along with her mother to study ballet too. Their living room was converted into a practice studio with a ballet bar and a gigantic gilt-framed mirror. Close to it Fitzgerald tried to write; he was irritated by the record that Zelda played over and over during her stint of four or five hours a day.

Zelda had barely started work when, according to one of the biographies, she wrote their friend Carl Van Vechten that she had joined the Philadelphia Opera ballet. In the same letter she spoke of having found enough chaos—she liked the word chaos in those years—to go her own way, and that she was heading for Paris in the spring to study ballet. To reduce the tensions between them, Fitzgerald closed the house and they went to Paris.

"She was soon lost to the ballet craze," he said about that period in their lives.

Paris was the dance capital after the Russian Revolution sent most of the dancers into exile. Many groups had settled there, and old dancers of the Russian ballet had opened studios to teach and coach.

One of these was Madame Lubov Egorova, a former princess and ballerina, who had taught Miss Littlefield and also a daughter of Fitzgerald's friends the Murphys.

"Zelda had to study with Egorova—the teacher who would turn her into a ballerina with a magic wand," he said with a note of bitterness. "We met her at one of Gerald's parties. They entertained the Diaghilev company. But that wasn't the year Zelda was stung by the ballet bug. Of course she had taken dancing lessons before, and sometimes she kicked off her slippers and let herself go into a solo. In her absorbed state she ignored the applause of friends and strangers.

"Yes, I saw plenty of ballet dancers because of her. They live in a fairy-tale world of their own making, detached from life and reality. I saw them as children taking silly poses and with as much common sense as a third-rate Italian tenor. Ballet was a mystical experience to them, and their teacher was a saint to worship. That was the worst atmosphere for Zelda in her chaotic mental state. She threw herself into it with the blind faith and adoration of a child."

They were in Paris a part of that year and returned the next for her to continue with Egorova, or so I learned later. That second year Diaghilev died and, though Nijinsky had been confined to an institution for more than a decade, dancers there were lamenting the end of the ballet. Zelda had a couple of minor engagements on the Riviera, and she also received an offer from the enterprising San Carlo Opera ballet school in Naples, but rejected it. Yet this attention gave her the illusion that she was professional and ready for the big time. She now worked harder than ever with Egorova; she was dieting for her figure and she put on grease paint for her ballet class. Fitzgerald said she was drinking too, to sustain her long practice periods, the hours with Egorova in class, and private lessons. Ballet became her obsession; neither he nor Scottie existed, only her teacher who possessed the gift to turn her into a ballerina.

"Zelda wanted to shine like a big star in the most glamorous of all worlds, the dance world. I didn't mind, but there was something absurd and pathetic about her efforts," he said with sadness in his voice. "I found myself saying hateful things to her. I couldn't stop. I was at war with myself. We quarreled, poked in the ashes of the past, and flung words that raised a wall of indifference between us. We became hostile strangers and went our separate ways while living a hell under the same roof."

One day while Zelda lunched with friends before going to ballet

class, she showed definite signs of her first breakdown. She had cocktails, ate little, was nervous, possibly because of her dieting, and
feared being late, although she had plenty of time to make her class.
She left in a taxi, changing into practice clothes on the way; when the
cab stopped at a light she hopped out and dashed wildly on foot the
rest of the way. A few days later she entered a Paris hospital, where
the doctor diagnosed anxiety symptoms and advised her to stop the
lessons for a while. But she resumed them and two weeks later had
her first breakdown.

I was curious to know whether Fitzgerald remembered or had an
idea why she had started ballet in 1927 with Littlefield, instead of two
years earlier with Egorova. My question brought him to his feet. He
walked away from me, his step was heavy, and there was a slight
hunch to his shoulders. After a silence he turned to me as if he had
pondered my question, hit on something he hadn't expected, and
seemed undecided about telling me.

"That summer in Wilmington," he slowly said, walking toward me,
"there were signs of disaster in her craving for excitement. She was
bored, restless, irritable. She tried painting—it bothered her eyes.
Writing hadn't brought her the success she most wanted. There was
still ballet. It was now or never. I can't say she functioned with such
logic. Rather I'm inclined to believe that Zelda—in her chaotic state—
needed a shock to get her going."

A fixed expression was on his face. He stopped a short distance
from me and seemed to be debating with himself whether he should
tell me what had occurred to him. And then, even if he had decided
against it, he seemed incapable of holding back what was on his mind.

"That shock might have been the news of Isadora's fatal accident,"
he said in a low voice, while looking at me intently as though what he
said was meant only for my ears. "I'm not saying it was. Probably it
was a coincidence, or it's only one of my hunches. Yet it's possible.
She started to study ballet a bit sooner, but she didn't go into high
gear until mid-September, when the accident occurred. Isadora was
an extraordinary woman. One in the limelight, one she would like to
have been. Isadora did it on her own. It was Zelda's insane wish to do
the same. Replace Isadora now that she was dead, and outshine me at
the same time."

Then for the first time he briefly recounted how Zelda had flung
herself down the steps after he sat at Isadora's feet. The episode, he
said, was no fit of jealousy as he had thought at the time; Zelda was

too proud to show jealousy. It was an early symptom of her illness. He again hesitated before telling me the rest of the thoughts my question had stirred up.

"The day we heard the news of the accident, there was a severe, brooding look in Zelda's eyes. I can still—"

He stopped as though realizing the full significance of what he had said. He became fearful and suspicious that I might repeat it, and mentioned the fear to me. I assured him that I respected a confidence and that he had nothing to worry about. He may well have remembered that I hadn't divulged the name of the person who told me what he had done about *Save Me the Waltz*. I was, in fact, silent on both matters for thirty-five years. But a tag end of suspicion must have stayed in his mind.

Before I left him that afternoon, he had more to say about Zelda's breakdown, as if speaking about it gave him relief. When I went back I made notes in a rental copy of *Nijinsky;* I still have the copy in which I jotted down what Fitzgerald said to me:

"As a child Zelda dreamed of becoming a Pavlova. As a woman she worked madly to outshine Isadora. And on her road to insanity she followed the footsteps of Nijinsky. Ironic. She had more in common with him then than during his shining years. They both had a daughter and wished for another child, a son. They wrote at great speed under pressure of their madness. They spent time at Valmont clinic where their illness was diagnosed by Professor Eugen Bleuler, foremost authority on schizophrenia, who believes that no one can become insane, but is born to it. And they both turned to God and religion in the fantasy world of dreams. A full circle for Zelda.

"To this day I feel partly responsible for her breakdown, though experts have told me that her trouble started long before we met. But this much I know for certain. She may have shown signs of insanity those first years, but she didn't crack up until she cut me out of her life and went over to Egorova and her crowd of ballet mystics. Throughout our years together, I gave Zelda a kind of balance that kept her from going over the brink. I was her only reality. Yes . . . I was her only reality."

22

Fitzgerald seriously tried to discipline himself and stay on the wagon. But there was a story to finish and he couldn't do it on beer; his creative imagination had been conditioned to stronger stuff. A drink of gin could turn the trick. After some deliberation, he took it and the story was quickly dispatched. It gave him such a boost that he took another and then another.

I saw him the day that he received a wire from Rosemary's doctor with the news that she had been committed to a mental hospital. He was drinking but seemed calm and in control, proud that he could stop at the limit he had set for himself. I noticed that he wasn't upset by the news about Rosemary; at an earlier time this might have plunged him into a fit of depression. He seemed to take it as an expected event, after his experience with Zelda.

"Women. Nature built them to perform the most menial and difficult tasks." He spoke with a light sneer on his stern, thin lips, and with an overconfident air. "They bear children, put up with years of boredom, and send men to an early grave. But nature played them a dirty trick. She endowed them with a weak nervous system. Their bodies can take it, but their nerves break, and they collapse, while men go on plodding to pay the bills. I'm very impatient with sick people —except Zelda. She's my invalid."

Fitzgerald had received two letters from Rosemary before she went to the hospital. One informed him that her sister had had a breakdown. The other letter was pitiful; she wouldn't accept the fact that their affair was something to be listed among "items to be forgotten." Probably he should have answered and encouraged her to accept her former life. Though grateful to Rosemary for the liberating effect of her love, he said that she was a distant memory.

"I was mistaken about her, as I've been about other women," he added with the same detachment. "I thought she was strong and could take this kind of experience without breaking—even if I was her first. She had all the confidence of beauty, youth, wealth, but was weak. I hate weakness and particularly the show of it. I despise it in myself and I have on occasion shown surprising strength. It's as if I were under hypnosis. I come up with the strength of a weak man. That keeps me going, along with fear and necessity."

Strength and vitality were qualities he sought in his friends. He once said that he kept seeing me because I possessed them; and yet he seemed irritated by my show of radicalism, my taste for the sort of writing he scorned as barnyard stuff, and my active interest in Negro rights. This might not have annoyed him so much if I had been a bit of a drinker or a less independent and more pliable friend, one to echo his opinions on literature and politics. No doubt my attitude was partly responsible for the gulf that had recently become evident in our friendship.

As the distance grew wider between us, I learned from Lottie that she and Fitzgerald were seeing each other more and more. By habit and profession she was a night owl. Free at the oddest hours, she became a convenient companion for his sleepless nights when no one else was available and she happened to call him. Their friendship was sealed when she went to see him—out of pity or worry—because she couldn't get him off her mind. She had found him sober and most gracious; he apologized like a boy, begging forgiveness for having slapped her, and he convinced her of his sincerity.

He always found women more manageable, sympathetic, and appealing to his nature than men, and he made no secret of preferring their company. He could tell them his troubles and weep on their shoulders; they showed him tenderness and warmth. He could speak of his duty toward Zelda and his daughter; they respected his strong family sentiment and sense of duty. He could explain the sexual ideas of Freud and Lawrence or the philosophies of Marx and Spengler, and they were impressed as though he were a brilliant young college professor. If he felt the sudden urge for sex, he often found them ready to oblige.

For a man whose morale was at an all-time low, he was fortunate in being a celebrated writer—even if he was in eclipse—pursued by attractive young women. He had kept away from prostitutes for moral reasons, and fears of disease, and this was possibly the only time in his life that he had contact with a professional. Lottie asked for nothing, accepted trifles, and didn't complicate his life. Their relationship proved more satisfactory and safer, he said, than casual affairs he had had in the past.

For the rest of the year in Asheville, I was to see less of Fitzgerald and more of Lottie—because of him. He was out of town days and a week at a time, and so was she; but I had no reason to think they went off together or met somewhere and, if they did, not even she told me. Now when I saw Fitzgerald he barely mentioned her, and when I saw Lottie she was always eager to talk about him.

It was sometime in August that I noticed the change Lottie had undergone since meeting Fitzgerald, particularly when she spoke about him. She wasn't the actress, cool and flippant, but more like a young woman who had discovered feelings and emotions and was enjoying them. Also there was a note of shyness about her that I hadn't expected to see in a woman of her worldly experience.

She gave me that impression late one evening in the bookshop. I was typing a book column when I heard a tapping on the glass, as I had the night I met Fitzgerald. At first I barely recognized her; she wore a dark gown with gold trimmings and an orange chiffon scarf wrapped loosely about her head and shoulders. I opened the door with surprise and she swept in like a young woman on her way to a dance.

"Hi," she said, a bit breathless.

"Hi—" It was all I could say.

"Juliet and Romeo are at the Château and a gent's sending his car for me." She noticed my surprise at seeing her dressed up at such an hour. "You're working. I'll only be here a bit."

"I'm glad to see you, Lottie," I said, switching on another light so I could see her better. There was something fresh and lovely about her, and she bore little resemblance to the woman I knew who peddled her body. "You look great."

"So you like this?" she said with a frown and went through the motions of unrolling the frothy material off her head. "It's his idea. This gent's taking me to a country club and will pass me off as an old sweetheart."

"You don't look that old." I laughed.

"To hell with him," she said, tossing the scarf on a chair. Her face took on a grave look and her eyes met mine. "But turn out that light. I've got to tell you about your friend."

She said that Fitzgerald was her first affair since she gave up the theater. She found him to be fun and exciting, charming and lovable when sober, nasty and abusive when drunk. But she excused him as she might have excused a spoilt youngster, saying that she enjoyed catering to his whims and minor vanities. Then she launched into what she had learned of his inadequacy as a lover.

"The boys called him a sissy when he went to school dressed up like Little Lord Fauntleroy," she said with a swishy gesture. "He liked to dress up, but had to prove he was a real boy. So he went in for football and fights in a big way. Losing seemed to spur him on. He tried at prep school and college too. There he switched to the theater. He had a picture taken when he was playing a pretty showgirl in a musical. It was in a New York paper. A burlesque house offered him a job as a female impersonator. Maybe Minsky's. His good looks sometimes were embarrassing. His pet hate is fairies—and for good reason."

He had told her of the time when Zelda said that he was a fairy so forcefully that he almost believed it. Of course, Lottie said, his inability to satisfy her had much to do with it. At the time, he and Zelda were trying to have another baby. His failure bothered him; he told Lottie he had tried with other women who wanted a child by him, and met with no better luck. That summer he saw a specialist, who decided that his rundown physical state, aggravated by poor nutrition, insomnia, sleeping pills, too much drinking, and too many problems, had contributed to his inadequacy and weakened his reproductive capacity so that he might never again become a father.

Most of his adult life he had tried to prove that he was a man, Fitzgerald told her. Though he didn't possess masculine appeal, he had good looks, intelligence, and understood the nature of women. Now he wanted to please them—if he could overcome the harm his wife had done in berating him for his size and for being "a lousy lover." Late one night he confided to Lottie that he believed the real reason for his hasty climax was fear and guilt, both going back to his boyish years of masturbating, a time when he thought sex was dirty and sinful.

"Your friend was a virgin when he met his wife—he's not sure about her and was faithful to her until that affair with the French aviator. That—" she hesitated a moment—"almost wrecked him. He needs alcohol to give him confidence and get over his fears. It makes him sexy and nasty at times. He wants to prove he's a man but he's overdone it. There have been fifty or sixty women, so he says, and one night when he couldn't sleep he made a list. He said he graded them for looks, age, profession, social position, shape of breasts and feet, and whether single, married, or divorced.

"But he's not one to kid himself, thinking he's a Casanova with all those conquests. He knows it's because of his fame, talent, and good looks and not for any sexual prowess. These adoring females are chasing the famous writer. He calls himself a sort of *'homme fatal.'* " Lottie paused. In the semidarkness I saw an aged, concerned look on her face. "I've thought about him a lot. I'm doing what I can to help him over his worst fault as a lover. But his biggest problem's to prove to himself he's a man. And I hope I can convince him about—"

"Lottie—" I said after a short silence. I wondered whether she had become seriously interested in him. She struck me for the first time as a woman of feeling and understanding. I wanted to warn her not to get involved, and then I decided she was smart enough to know men and what she wanted.

Lottie went on to tell me that he had mentioned a feminine trait in his make-up which seemed to invite women to pursue him. This was the reverse of the accepted custom of men pursuing women; and he explained that it showed he was the weaker and more passive partner while the woman was the stronger and more active one. This had been the situation of his gentle father and dominant mother, and it might have been partly responsible for his own compliant role in relationships—a role he shared with some of his male characters.

"That romantic sap Gatsby," she added, as though it had just occurred to her. Now she smiled, rose, and paced the shop, saying that Fitzgerald had decided to do something about her lack of literary knowledge. He had spent a night lecturing her on the English poets. Keats was his favorite, and he recited two of his odes to her. She didn't understand them, though they sounded tender and romantic—the way he sounded to her.

"He said it was a shame I didn't know any of the beautiful poems in our language and it'd please him to help me make their acquaintance. He said I mustn't think I was stupid because I couldn't understand them. There's one he said he's read a hundred times. You believe it?"

I nodded. "The 'Ode to a Nightingale.' "

"That's it," she said, stopping before me. "But I haven't figured out where the nightingale comes in."

"You will."

It seemed that his interest in her went further than improving her education. He had also touched on her profession. She was bright and lovely, he said, and it sickened him to think she was selling her body.

"It's degrading," he said to her. "Can't you take up nursing, be a waitress, a cashier?"

She then spoke of his interest in an English writer named Lawrence, whose books he had told her to read. "Do you have any?" she asked.

I took four books from the shelves and placed them before her.

"But you might find them too long and dull," I said. "Why not try Hemingway?"

"Hemingway? That friend his wife accused him about?" she asked and put down the books. "What kind does he write?"

"Love, drinking, bull fighting, and hunting. Tough talk and lots of action. He-man stuff."

"He would."

"Try this—if you want Lawrence," I said and handed her the pirated (and expurgated) edition of *Lady Chatterley's Lover* from behind the desk.

"What's it about?"

"Love."

"Is that all writers think about?"

23

That summer Fitzgerald sometimes spoke of his need for corresponding with friends; letters kept him from feeling forgotten and out of touch with the world. Regardless of his mental or physical state he wrote to two friends in particular, his agent Harold Ober and his editor Maxwell Perkins; he wrote to Zelda, who needed cheering up, and to Scottie, who needed fatherly counseling as she neared fourteen. He was concerned about her adolescent problems, seeing himself as her sole guide because of Zelda's illness.

He preferred women's company but there were times when he wanted someone with whom he could discuss books, writers, and contemporary events. The bookshop, which reminded him of his early days in St. Paul, and my *Contempo* background served as his link in Asheville with such a world. And though he did most of the talking and was plainly irritated by my youthful convictions, he seemed to need a critical and questioning companion as much as a pliable and adoring one. As our old intimacy faded, he spoke less of his troubles and more about literature, radical friends, and writers since the turn of the century.

One day in the bookshop, during one of his short dry spells, he said that Shane Leslie and H. G. Wells had influenced him more than Compton Mackenzie or Booth Tarkington. Mackenzie's *Sinister Street* had nevertheless served as one of the models for *This Side of Paradise*, and Tarkington's Penrod was supposed to have started him writing about his own youth as Basil (in stories some of which were reprinted in *Taps at Reveille*). Leslie and Wells appealed to his inner nature; they were social thinkers and moralists rather than entertaining storytellers.

Fitzgerald mentioned two of Leslie's books that interested him as a

137

young writer of Irish heritage, *End of a Chapter* and *Celts of the World.* Like his friend Monsignor Fay, Leslie was an aesthete and a Catholic convert; they had both tried to keep him in the bosom of the church. Ten years before the Soviet revolution, Leslie had gone to Russia and there had become a friend of Tolstoi, whose social philosophy appealed to him. At King's College, Cambridge, he was involved with Christian Socialism and the Irish literary renaissance. Leslie also wrote a college novel, which Fitzgerald said was withdrawn in the mid-twenties because of objections by Cambridge.

Speaking of Wells, Fitzgerald reminded me that his *Ann Veronica* was the novel he had chosen to represent the prewar generation, which, in his opinion, fancied itself modern but was strongly attached to Victorian traditions. As I had not read *Ann Veronica*, he told me that it was the first popular English novel in which a heroine was allowed to show honesty of desire and have sexual freedom. Ann was a virgin who chose a lover instead of waiting, as was customary, for a man to choose her.

"The book created a scandal and was banned in the libraries," he said. "It was a moral offense for an English girl to be sex-conscious before a man had awakened desire in her. Some called her a whore, and Wells lost most of his friends, except Shaw and Chesterton. After Ann, heroines like her began to appear in dozens of novels and by the thousands in real life. Things were never the same in the British Empire or in English popular fiction."

While he spoke I thought of his flappers ten years later, who were called "speed" for kissing and necking with boys. I wanted to ask him why American popular fiction was shackled by Victorian taboos later than the English, but he went on to talk about Wells's *The New Machiavelli*, which he considered another literary milestone in presenting a girl's uninhibited passion. Macmillian refused to publish it, and Wells's socialist friends called him "the Fabian Casanova."

"Feminists who had joined the Fabian Socialists to push for women's rights turned their backs on Wells. The only right they wanted was the right to vote. When it came to opinions about sex, the feminists wanted nothing to do with him. He said they were mostly Victorian women whose modesty went deeper than their boldness as modern rebels. Wells's novels are more cerebral than emotional, and they influenced the young generation as the plays of Shaw and Ibsen did."

He then spoke of Joyce and Stein, two of his literary idols, though their work was becoming increasingly difficult for him to understand. Both owed a great deal to avant-garde magazines such as *The Transat-*

lantic Review, transition, or *The Little Review* for making them known as the baffling revolutionaries of the word. He was puzzled that Joyce and Stein did not meet for a long time and that, when they were introduced at a Jo Davidson party in Paris, they had exchanged less than a dozen words. "Banalities," Fitzgerald said. "I think Stein said that they lived in the same Parisian quarter and Joyce said that their names were often linked together. And then they shut up like clams. I know Joyce shunned her—but why?"

"Perhaps Joyce couldn't bear the sight of her anymore than Braque could," I ventured to explain. "Braque thought that Stein and Toklas were like a pair of carnival freaks." Remembering something I had recently read, I added, "Also Stein has a gift for self-advertising. If Joyce were to be seen with her, it might give the impression that she had influenced him as she had done Anderson, Hemingway, and you, perhaps in a different way from the development of style, rhythm, and—"

I stopped abruptly, and I remember his searching gaze.

"Why do you say that?"

"Call it a hunch, as you might say. Stein had a way of creating such an impression—if she didn't come right out and claim credit. Such as discovering painters, being intimately involved with the origins of Cubism, Dada, Surrealism, and *transition.* I know there are petty quarrels over such things, as in that Cowley-Munson controversy over *Secession,* but anyhow Stein gives that impression in her Toklas autobiography."

"Wasn't Stein mixed up with all that stuff?"

I went to the desk and dug out a pamphlet published that February as a *transition* supplement and handed it to him. It was entitled "The Testimony Against Gertrude Stein" and was signed by Braque, Matisse, André Salmon, Tristan Tzara, and Eugene and Maria Jolas. They offered facts to show that Stein had only a superficial knowlege of all the movements she claimed a role in. Tzara, who had fathered Dada, said that her connection with art was due solely to money. Braque declared that she completely misunderstood Cubism, and that none of the painters had known about her until she appeared in *transition.* Mme. Jolas, whose husband had founded the magazine, told the story of its origins and editorship.

Fitzgerald didn't care who founded *transition* or how little Stein knew about modern art, but he was concerned over Stein's angry feelings toward Jolas for using less and less of her work and more and more of Joyce's. At the time, Jolas was publishing portions of *Work in*

Progress, which was to become *Finnegans Wake*. When Stein reproached Jolas for neglecting her in favor of Joyce, she is reported to have said, "Why do you continue to lay emphasis on the work of that fifth-rate Irish politician?"

"Probably there is something to your hunch. It bears out what Ernest told me about Stein and his decision to quit being her pupil," Fitzgerald said, slowly handing back the pamphlet. "There was a somewhat similar situation between Ernest and me when he was writing *The Sun*. He didn't want me to read it until it was finished, thinking I might take credit for making suggestions. But when I did make them he was too good a writer to ignore them. Instead of bringing us closer, this led to his growing coolness that I told you about."

I set aside the pamphlet and picked up a *Contempo* I wanted him to see because of its review of *Death in the Afternoon*. It was entitled "I Come Not to Bury Hemingway" and was written by Henry Hart. The passage that interested Fitzgerald read, "The inevitable human necessity of smashing the idol that has been worshiped now appears against Hemingway. His time had come, he had served his purpose, the novelty he supplied had become familiar. There was now a need to get even with the object of adulation. Smashing the idol and spitting into the Hemingway legend consisted of getting up and saying, 'Poor Hem! He's made a big show of being virile. The world has passed him by.' Then the Max Eastman crack, 'We know you, Hemingway. Take that false hair off your chest!' It is true that Hemingway served his purpose. . . . In his stripped prose there is the staccato beat of hope. . . .

"There are two things he profoundly believes in. One is that it is his fate to perceive what tragedy does to people, what it makes them do, and how it leaves them, and that because of this no personal tragedy to himself can ever happen that would be anything other than another occurrence for him to observe. The second thing he believes in profoundly is having a good time and in changing whatever you are doing when it no longer makes you feel good. This is important from the standpoint of vitality. . . ."

Fitzgerald looked up and said, "I served my purpose and am finished. But I can't believe Ernest's vital talent will fade during his lifetime or his work will be neglected like mine now that its novelty is gone. He is a finished artist. A genius. Our friendship is one of the high points of my life. I'm sorry we won't see much of each other again. It's my fault as much as his. But it's a shame success seems to have gone to his head, as it did to mine when I was a cocky, arrogant youth and landed on top."

This led him to speak of changing trends in fiction, a subject that concerned him a lot that summer. He noticed in *Contempo* two writers who were striking examples of the new and the old. The old was James Branch Cabell, whose erudite fable *Jurgen* was the modish book of the early twenties and who had recently made his appearance simply as Branch Cabell. The new writer was Nathanael West, whose realistic fable *Miss Lonelyhearts* was admired by intellectuals during the mid-thirties.

He was both annoyed and pleased that we had published, two years earlier, an obit on Cabell; annoyed because Cabell was a friend of Mencken's and Nathan's, and pleased because no young writers were trying to imitate him. In a recent book Cabell had given a trumpet call to announce his own demise. Our article stated that he would have been dead from the first—if the censor hadn't fumed against *Jurgen*'s merry eroticism and made the book notorious and fashionable by trying to suppress it.

"Zelda knew Cabell's novels before I did. She would break into wild fits of laughter while reading *Jurgen*. I didn't read it until the winter after we were married. Then I thought it was second-rate Anatole France. Cabell was very kind to *Gatsby* and *The Beautiful and Damned*. I was lucky to hit it with my first book. Cabell made it after years of comparative neglect—and you bury him while he's still alive and turning out a book a year. I admit that's too many, but I know what it is to be buried in one's lifetime."

He turned to the space we had given West and *Miss Lonelyhearts*. We had run an excerpt prior to book publication, then four articles praising the novel, and a personal portrait by his brother-in-law, S. J. Perelman. One of the reviews was by William Carlos Williams, another by Bob Brown. "West is a bright new talent. I hope he doesn't get buried under that avalanche of novels about the great unwashed and exploited American masses."

He directed a sardonic look at me as I went to answer the phone. I couldn't be sure whether he meant what he was saying or was simply trying to get a rise out of me. When I rejoined him, his thoughts were elsewhere and he was somewhat sad.

"Know anything about Ted Coy?"

"I don't think I do."

"I thought so." He turned on me sharply, so sharply that I withdrew a step or two. "That's the trouble with you radicals. You know about art and literature, cuckoo magazines, anarchism, communism, Sacco and Vanzetti, Mooney and Billings, the Five Year Plan, Dada, and the coming revolution, but you don't know a God-damned thing about football!"

I almost laughed but didn't, knowing it would have made him more furious.

"Ted Coy, if anybody asks you, was one of our greatest athletes," he said like a patient schoolmaster. "He's Ted Fay, Basil's godlike football hero in 'The Freshest Boy,' and I used him in other characters. He was married to Jeanne Eagles."

"I know her," I was happy to say. "Sadie Thompson in *Rain*. I went daffy about her in *The Letter*, One of the most—"

"It's Ted I want you to know about and remember. He was one of my heroes." Fitzgerald looked away and, after a silence, added in a restrained voice, "Ted died a couple of days ago. A heart attack. Forty-seven, bankrupt, and forgotten except by his teammates, sportswriters, and fans like me."

He bowed his head, walked out of the bookshop, and marched off as though bringing up the rear of a street funeral.

24

Indeed, the death of his football hero that September deeply affected Fitzgerald, as that of his close friend Ring Lardner had done two years before. These were signs that an era was over and that he was doomed with it. His resolve to start a new life had received a setback when he switched from beer back to gin for the sake of his writing. He was now drinking with no pretense of rationing himself, as though Ted Coy's inglorious end had dashed all hope of his attempt to rise from the depths.

When I next saw him at the Inn, his face was pallid, his eyes were strained, his hands so shaky he could scarcely light a cigarette without cursing under his breath. There was still a touch of eczema on his body, but he had lost weight now that he was drinking less beer. He greeted me with a frown and seemed annoyed about something. I was sorry I had come out to see him.

"You have kept me waiting."

"I'm sorry. The bus—"

"I didn't say you *kept* me waiting," he corrected. "I said you *have* kept me waiting. Any school kid knows the difference."

"Of course," I said, more baffled than intimidated.

"Skip it. I suppose it doesn't matter to a press agent. You fellows speak a jargon of your own."

He offered me a drink, which I refused, and then quoted a line out of *Tender Is the Night:* "If you spend your life sparing people's feelings and feeding their vanities, you get so you can't distinguish what should be respected in them."

I thought I got the point, but he went on to explain it in another light.

"The moment you spare people's feelings, you're no longer worthy of their friendship. You can't do ballyhoo without feeding vanity with

143

a ladle. And as for losing that sense of what to respect, you've lost contact with the best in them, and you've become a fraud."

I wondered what I had said or done that called for this short lecture. I could only think of a conversation we once had about my learning press-agentry. What he had said about publicity was to remain with me for life; a day rarely passed that I didn't remember his contempt for the craft and those who practiced it. "A press agent is a hack turned huckster. A front man who serves the vanities of his clients and the vagaries of newspaper people. He can never be himself, only a shadow of those he serves. He's their whipping boy, a tax deduction, a glorified pimp on their expense accounts."

Fitzgerald went to the couch and partly stretched out on it. I sat in a chair facing him. He now spoke of his life cycle—drink, sex, work. A cigarette stub was burning out in an ash tray near me. I crushed it. He frowned at me as though I had done something awful.

"You don't smoke, drink, know a damn about sports, or whore around—and you can't stand a put-out cigarette. Sometimes I wonder if you're not a sissy."

He knew as well as I did that all those things had nothing to do with being a sissy. I said nothing, but I was thinking I shouldn't have come, even if he had sounded lonely and depressed on the phone. He was now flipping the pages of Robert Forsythe's *Redder Than the Rose*, which he had asked me to bring him. It was a collection of pieces, mostly about literary, stage, and screen personalities; many of these first appeared in *The New Masses*.

"You must know he's Kyle Crichton of *Collier's*," he said with less annoyance.

"Yes, but I never read him in *Collier's*."

"I haven't read him in the *Masses*. I believe he was an assistant editor of *Scribner's Magazine*, and he worked as a young man in Pennsylvania mines and mills. No barnyard dude, but a writer who comes to his radicalism honestly. He has the gift of not letting his right hand know what his left is doing. Probably I should've used two names—my own for serious writing and another for the cheap stuff."

"But he gets nothing from the *Masses*," I said.

"Of course, he does it for the Cause," he said with a note of scorn. "You like him, don't you?"

"He's a hilarious writer. Takes a swipe at some of your friends. Wilson for saying communism is too good for the communists. Stein, who claims she's redder than all the reds. Hemingway, Woollcott, Mencken."

"I want to see what he says about Ernest and Mencken."

"Page one for Mencken. And you're in it."

Fitzgerald slowly opened the book. By that time he had gotten over most of Mencken's influence. He seemed pleased by the remark. "It is probably accurate to say that he [Mencken] was a case of arrested youth but there is something appealing in the sight of a man of forty-five keeping as much alive as a Princeton junior who has been reared on the works of F. Scott Fitzgerald." He turned to the Hemingway piece, which began, "Quite the most delicate thing in the world is an author and quite the most delicate of authors is Mr. Hemingway. . . ." After reading a bit, he turned more pages, read more, and was silent.

"Wit is as rare in the radical press as an original idea," he said with a thoughtful look. "Its writers have more venom than style, no sense of proportion, and are soaked in Party clichés. Another of their gifted writers is Michael Gold. He blasted Thornton Wilder and his cult in *The New Republic*. You must've read it."

"I missed it," I said. "Mike visited us in Chapel Hill after Langston Hughes came to read his poetry and shortly before Faulkner showed up. He promised to send me a copy. I never got it."

"I was surprised to see him in *The New Republic*. But I shouldn't have been. Bunny was on it, along with a crowd that reads like your masthead—Waldo Frank, Lewis Mumford, Malcolm Cowley. The review was a Marxist social and economic interpretation of Wilder, and Bunny defended part of it in an editorial. I remember mostly Gold's rehash of the theme of *The Theory of the Leisure Class*, which Veblen wrote around 1900."

The Leisure Class, Fitzgerald said, was one of his favorite books. Veblen foresaw the course that American culture would follow after our period of expansion and prosperity. Spengler would call it a money culture twenty-five years later. So Gold had a point when he spoke of Wilder as the perfect flowering of that new prosperity, and the poet of that recently risen class in America—the genteel bourgeoisie. His novels have what Veblen said the leisure class would need to gratify its desire for good breeding, smartness, mobility, and its love for the artistic and the archaic.

"Of course, it's only a veneer, but the parvenu class sorely needed such a paint job to cover up its lowly origins, to forget the source of its wealth from cutthroat business and industrialism, to create the illusion of having an aristocratic sensivity, and to give the impression of being worthy of its fortunes. But Wilder is more of a writer than

Gold was willing to grant. Bunny says he owes a great debt to Proust and is his American popularizer. I like his *Cabala* more than *The Bridge of San Luis Rey*, but I found *Woman of Andros* as much a mediocrity as Steinbeck's latest."

Fitzgerald poured himself another drink from the bottle. With each glass his voice sounded fuzzier. He recalled a psychiatrist in Switzerland who wanted him to undergo therapy to cure his drinking. But he declined, saying he was already too analytical and the psychoanalytical method would destroy the best of his talent, which he believed sprang from his intuition and the deep reservoir of his emotions.

"I know writers who bogged down and never wrote a decent line after analysis. All they could echo was Freud, Jung, and Lawrence—half-baked," he added as he attempted to light a cigarette. I tried to steady his hand with mine; he pushed it aside with a scornful look. "I couldn't risk having my unconscious examined. I believe Jung says it can be fatal in some cases. Besides, drinking is one of the three pleasures I have left. Now about this psychiatrist—the hell with him," he stopped, holding me with a hostile stare, "there's something more urgent."

I again thought I shouldn't have come. His voice sounded thicker and more quarrelsome and he was back in his earlier mood. While he had been thinking of Veblen, Wilder, Gold, Crichton, and his friend Bunny, I had felt at ease. Now I could see he was heading for another outburst. He was silent a moment as he rubbed his hands and blindly stared at them.

"I told you—you *have kept* me waiting," he said without looking at me. "Probably you don't know it. When I want something, I want it now. I must know something. No more stalling. The truth—all of it—the worst as you see it. The worst and I are a grand old couple. What's going to happen to me?"

He flung his expressive hands before me and opened shaky palms. I slowly took them. I had avoided reading them for fear of saying something that might annoy or upset him. Now I had to read them or he might become still more hostile.

Considering the mood he was in, I couldn't tell him the worst. I can't recall what or how much I told him. I edited my remarks, as I had sometimes done in reading other hands, when I feared that their owners were too emotional or impressionable. Yet I remember his hands as the most perfect example of the Intuitive type. Their shape and markings are fixed in my memory, much as are some of his words and gestures. There are people who look upon palmistry with more or less justified skepticism, but it does offer clues to character. Fitzgerald, Zelda, Isadora, and a host of others believed in it firmly.

Fitzgerald had large, agile hands with soft, refined skin almost like a young woman's. His fingers were short compared with the long palm, which was covered by many fine, flamelike lines, grilles, and forks. The top phalanges were firm and the mounts robust and full. His lines of Mercury and Apollo were prominent, crossed by a partially balanced Girdle of Venus. The Life line was average and durable, extending into the Jupiter finger; the Heart line broad and fringed, while the Head line was comparatively short, and they were joined by the Croix Mystique.

Those were the main features I remember and they indicated what we already know—a highly creative temperament and personality. He possessed contradictory traits which at times kept him from producing his best work or maintaining a single balanced character. The signs indicated that his imagination, energy, and stubborn determination were gifts from his mother rather than from his father, who endowed him with his weakness, a kind of gentility, and a sense of failure.

He was a feeling rather than a thinking man, with deep stores of emotional energy. His basic conflict seemed to rise from an overactive conscious self at war with a highly developed unconscious. The outer events of his life—wild and extravagant as they seemed—were insignificant compared with the ferment of his inner self that found expression in his writing. With his inability to bring both into balance, he was bound to be an extremist and to waste energy, all of which motivated his lifelong preoccupation with emotional bankruptcy.

His Mount of Venus suggested warmth, generosity, and deep affection; that he was more aesthetic than physical, responding to sexuality through momentary passion and lust, but more satisfactorily through his imagination. His Luna bulged with romance, idealism, and beauty; he was more fanciful than realistic, more poet than novelist. The lines of Apollo and Mercury pointed up his intuition and brilliance, which were strengthened by small markings. While there were three or four relationship lines, one towered above the others.

Shy and deeply introverted, Fitzgerald needed a stimulant to free him from his inhibitions, and at such times he could turn into a brash and uncontrollable extrovert. Despite his self-involvement, he had the curiosity and humanity to seek out people—to charm, amuse, and stimulate. But socializing took its toll by inciting him at times to commit senseless and outrageous acts—an involuntary reaction for having forced himself into the acceptable form of behavior.

For all his outward success, Fitzgerald lacked a sense of genuine security. He was never quite sure of himself, he never could believe he was a top writer. He might boast at times that he was, but he swung from heights of self-confidence to depths of suicidal despair, with periods of calm in between to guide and sustain him. He had the signs of a hypersensitive temperament with a highly overdeveloped sense of inferiority.

Though he was a man divided, Fitzgerald was still able to function as a writer driven by ambition, fear, and necessity. He had more control over his talent than over his emotions, his energy, or his money. He was both observer and participator, analytical, with a mania for artistic perfection. He had markings of fame and fortune, but also a temperament which doomed him to see himself as a failure. He was what might be called a natural schizo—an artist at war with himself and the world around him.

"What about my lousy lungs?" he asked, as I summed up the reading on an optimistic note.

"They're not as lousy as you think," I said and traced his Life line with my thumbnail.

"How long?"

"You've been floundering on an island," I said, ignoring his question, "but there's a—"

"Damn it, I asked you, how long have I got?"

"Mark Twain and Sarah Bernhardt had your type of hand and they—"

"I'm no gilly!" He glared and jerked his hand from my grasp. "I told you not to spare me. I have hunches. I know the worst. I can take it too. Keep your press-agent lies!"

He rose, erect and furious, and stalked away as if he had caught me cheating. I was stunned by his sudden rage. I got up and went to the door. I turned to say good-by, but his back was to me. I left the place very much distressed, thinking I might never see him again.

Yes, I had spared him. His Life line was an average one, with signs of a deteriorating heart. His heart was a good one, but it had been weakened by his incurable habits and impossible life style. He had spoken of the human constitution as an amazing machine, which went out of commission when the heart had run its race. I expected his to run its race for another ten years, not to falter as soon as it did in fact—five years later.

Why didn't I tell him what I saw—as a warning?

It is a question I asked myself for years. Then I decided that there was no warning him. Fitzgerald's course was that of a man committed. He wouldn't have listened any more than Archy, my friend the Human Fly, would have listened to the gypsy. I remembered what Fitzgerald had said when he heard that story: "He never could have scaled that pole again. That would have been a more tragic end for him than crashing in his act."

L ottie dropped by one morning to tell me that she was
worried about his health.
Fitzgerald had caught a cold and said it could go into pleurisy because
of his scarred lungs. His breathing came hard and he spoke of a fever;
she had noticed that his eyes were glassy and his forehead was moist.
Despite her pleading there was no getting him into bed or keeping
him from the bottle, and he wouldn't let her call a doctor.

"Call him or go and see him," she said, concerned. "He needs
help."

"I will, but don't worry," I said. "He has a hell of a constitution.
One minute he's at the undertaker's and the next he's ready for anything."

"He looks awful."

"But did it keep him from talking?" I smiled to cheer her up, for
she was truly worried about him.

"No," she replied in a lighter tone. "He talked about his daughter
this time. It was my fault, I suppose, because I asked what he meant
by saying that he didn't become a member of the human race till he
was fifteen and that it had cost him plenty. Well, the girl's thirteen,
cocky and boastful like he was then. He said it's bad enough for a
boy, but it can ruin a girl. He showed me a picture of her. She's
pretty. That worries him too. He kept saying, 'Lottie and Scottie.' "

"Lottie and Scottie," I repeated.

"He said pretty girls have a ten-year lead on less fortunate ones.
They attract boys easily but can't hold them—in the long race. He's
trying to tell her it's the quiet ones, pretty or not, who land the bright
young men. She can talk—something he thinks is as dangerous as
being pretty. She'll never make a good listener—what he thinks those
boys want. A sensible girl knows when to be silent, when to smile,

and when to laugh, but not too loud like her mother. If she has to show she's clever, they'll shy away from her. The bright young man wants a companion, not a rival who's trying to outshine him.

"When he told me she was losing her head over boys, I told him he didn't have to worry about her. She was doing okay," Lottie said with a smile. "But he says she's a softie—the way he was—and he doesn't want her to get hurt. He wants her to become hard as nails. And he wants to curb her cocky streak without squelching her self-confidence. She's selfish too, he says. That has to be knocked out of her while she's young. It was his trouble—the thing that cost him plenty."

Fitzgerald then explained to her what he had meant, saying that selfish people don't think there is anybody in the world except themselves. He had been such a boy, and he blamed his mother for spoiling him. Until he left home he didn't realize there were others to consider. He had found out the hard way—with tears, despair, and loneliness—and he wasn't sure that he had succeeded in getting over his selfish ways.

When Lottie asked him why he said she had joined the human race at five, he simply replied that it was her self-assurance, her ability to be herself, and her relaxed way with others. She had faced the realities without too much strain on herself. On the other hand, he had joined it so late that it took everything he had to tackle his burdens each morning he woke up. It was a matter of attitude, intensity, and of being oneself without too many illusions.

"You're hard and brittle like most of your generation," Fitzgerald said to her. "I thought Rosemary was, too. She turned out not to be. You're tough and can take it. I tried to be tough. It's the only way to survive. We must learn to swim—to dominate life—if we're worth a damn. Or under we go. The way I have and I hate myself for it."

"You think I dominate life?" she asked him.

"Yes—even if it's not the sort of life I approve of," he said to her. "I know it's silly to try and reform you. But I must confess, I have the passion of a reformer. A schoolmaster, too. Probably I should have taught, but I prefer to choose my pupils and teach them what little I've learned that might make life easier, fuller, and more enjoyable for them—if not for myself. I can't learn it myself. I'm hopeless and blind like an old dog.

"Whether or not you're happy with your present life, it wasn't forced on you. You chose it with your eyes wide open. When it becomes intolerable, you'll give it up and take another road—alone or perhaps with someone you love. A few nights ago I was thinking, I seem to ruin all the women who come into my life. They end up in some disaster. I don't want that happening to you.

"Fortunately you're too level-headed and tough for that, but I'm warning you. You've been exceedingly kind to me. So kind you could be—if you were soft enough—that proverbial girl with a heart of gold. Only a fool believes that sort ever existed. I could be one who does, but, at the same time, I can scoff at the notion like the rest. I have that much on Gatsby—the fellow you called a romantic—"

"I'm sorry I—"

"You're young, attractive, and independent. So don't worry about, or get yourself involved with, a hopeless drinker who doesn't practice what he preaches and wastes your nights reciting poetry."

"I love it," she told him. "I left school to go on the stage."

"At least it's better than boring you with my wretched problems and miserable state of health."

"Let me hear the 'Nightingale' again."

Fitzgerald took another drink and recited it for her in a voice deep with emotion. Then he asked her if she had heard of two first-rate books about Russia—*Ten Days That Shook the World* and *New Russia's Primer*. Of course she hadn't, and he proceeded to tell her about them. Some time earlier he had noticed them in the shop and spoken at length to me about John Reed, the author of the first book.

He told her that the *Primer* was written by a Russian engineer who had to be a poet to have such a style. It was the story of Russia's Five Year Plan, for schoolchildren in their early teens. As did no other book he had read, it clarified the difference between America's planless economy for profit and the Soviet's planned production for use.

"We've learned to produce a surplus, yet the stuff is being dumped, burned, or plowed under as fertilizer. And we have poverty in the midst of plenty," he said to her. "Russia cannot produce enough for its millions, but has a plan to try and feed all of them. We have learned to produce, the Russians to distribute. Some of the best brains in America are saying, if we could get the two systems together, we might lick the Depression in a year."

Then he spoke of John Reed, whom he called a young man of action. Fitzgerald said that he too had yearned to be such a man; to toughen himself and overcome his sense of fear. Before telling her about Reed, he mentioned other writers who had led exciting lives and had written about them. Two of them were familiar to her—

Hemingway and Jack London—but she hadn't heard of John Reed or his book about Russia.

"Reed was a Westerner like London. It seems the West produced some of our most talented and rebellious young men," Fitzgerald said. "He was the son of a federal marshal in Oregon, who prosecuted the lumber trust for destroying virgin forests out there and not replacing them with a single young tree."

"When I told him I was a Westerner too—southern California—he was pleased," Lottie said in an aside. "He had thought so, and said he took me for an actress before we met."

"He did," I nodded, thinking that Fitzgerald was right after all in his initial observation.

"He kidded me, saying I must've started as a Hollywood starlet because they grow on trees out there like oranges."

Lottie recalled that he had told her John Reed was also of the theater. As a founder of the Provincetown Players, he had acted in a Eugene O'Neill play and had written a play of his own that the Players produced. Before that, when he was at Harvard, he had done the lyrics for the Hasty Pudding show, as Fitzgerald had done others for a Triangle musical at Princeton. Reed was a poet, too, and was to become a famous journalist.

"Oh, he told me a lot about John Reed," Lottie said. Reed had been in Petrograd during the October Revolution and soon afterward had written *Ten Days That Shook the World*. Lenin himself had praised the book. It was translated into Russian by Lenin's wife and was widely used as a text in Russian schools. After spending more than a year in America, where he tried to organize a revolutionary party, Reed had gone back to Russia. He had caught typhus while serving as delegate to a Communist convention on the Caspian Sea and had died two or three weeks later in Moscow. He was given a hero's funeral and was buried under the Kremlin Wall.

"Reed died at thirty-three—not too young for a man of action, yet not too old," Scott said to Lottie. "He lived by his convictions. That's more than I can say for myself—at times. I cannot help but admire him, and I recommend his book to anyone who can read. I'm asking my daughter to read it. Eisenstein made a film of *Ten Days*. Before it was released here, American Federation of Labor officials were invited to censor it. Ironical. They're more anti-Soviet than the biggest Hollywood or Wall Street tycoon."

Lottie asked me if I had the books. I told her we did; she decided to pick up Reed when she dropped off *Lady Chatterley's Lover*. She found

Chatterley dull, as though Lawrence had just learned about sex, and was forcing herself to finish it. Her parting words concerned Fitzgerald and his political beliefs.

"Is he a communist?"

"I think at times he'd like to believe he's one because of his friends who are."

"He doesn't look the type," she said with a thoughtful look. "When I was an actress I met all kinds. He's too clean-cut—with that air of a Prince Charming."

"That role becomes him," I said, pleased with her observation. "He seems to believe that a sort of intellectual aristocracy ought to run things—not the people."

"Isn't that backward—for these times?"

Her question surprised me. It was the first political opinion I had heard Lottie express.

After she left I phoned Fitzgerald to ask how he felt and whether I could drop in and bring him something from downtown. He coughed and said, yes, by all means, apparently pleased that I had called. But he sounded low in spirits and out of sorts; he was furious with the manager for forbidding the bellhops to bring him anything stronger than beer. When Fitzgerald told him he used alcohol for medicinal purposes, the manager replied that he would furnish it if Fitzgerald's doctor called to say he should have it.

Fitzgerald asked me to bring him a bottle of gin, saying he needed it to sweat out a cold that had gone down to his chest. I didn't relish the idea of encouraging another binge, yet there was no way to see him without bringing the bottle. I bought one and took a bus to the Inn. It was a gray, windy day; fall was in the air and I was wearing a light topcoat. I felt self-conscious walking through the lobby with the wrapped bottle under my arm, so I hid it under my coat and strolled to the elevator.

Fitzgerald grabbed the bottle and didn't thank me. His face was feverish, his voice thick and guttural, and he had a deep chest cough. Lottie was right: he needed medical attention, but that was far from his mind. He opened the bottle, sloshed the gin into a water glass, and drank it down quickly—the way he shoveled down those meals of steak and mashed potatoes that he took at long intervals.

"The son of a bitch! He'll burn in hell before I show him a doctor's prescription." All his anger was directed at the manager; I felt relieved that it was no longer at me. "He said if I didn't like it, I could leave. I won't until I'm goddamn ready or I'm thrown out for punching him in the nose."

Fitzgerald said that he had been sleeping very little and that he was troubled by nightmares and hallucinations. Everything around him had taken on a menacing aspect, as if it were bent on jeering at him, punishing him, and making him aware of his sins. He had the recurring sensation of circling in space, then of finding himself in the jaws of a whirlpool and of being sucked deep into an underwater grave. He would come out of the nightmare in a cold sweat, gasping for air, his heart thumping against his chest.

"Last night I saw myself in a cage like a sad, big-eared baboon," he said in a voice that sounded strange to me, as though he were still under the spell of the nightmare. "People were throwing peanut shells and banana peelings at me. Then they lighted cigarettes and they told me to dance like a pickaninny. I had to dance to keep from burning my feet, but I couldn't keep it up. I collapsed in the flames and they kept jeering at me.

"There was something I can't remember. I must have been on the edge of consciousness when I saw myself again in the cage. The fire was out, I didn't have a single burn. A dozen people filed past, silent as ghosts, and sat before me like a frozen jury. An officer tapped my shoulder and pointed at someone who turned out to be a judge. He wore a flaming wig and long curls. I couldn't be sure whether it was a man or a woman. The face was a man's, the voice a woman's, and the body was shrouded in a purple robe, like Isadora's. She asked me by what right I could take love—love that belonged to others—and leave them shattered and ruined for life.

"The cage went up in flames and smoke. Again I had the sensation of circling in space, back in the jaws of the whirlpool, and being sucked into that liquid grave." He paused and pointed to a letter he had received that morning from Rosemary. "It says her husband had a heart attack. The poor bastard can't play golf any more. Rosemary and golf were all he lived for, and I robbed him of both. I destroy everybody who comes near me. Women's nerves break, men's hearts fail. Can't one of these nightmares finish me, or am I doomed to this punishment?"

His head sank into his hands and he was silent except for the cough and his deep breathing. Then he spoke of Lottie, saying he had warned her of his destructive effect on women who were close to him. She hadn't taken it seriously, and he had no idea whether he would see her again. Despite his depressed and chaotic state, he expressed a tender feeling for her, adding that she was one of the few women who hadn't burdened him with new problems.

"Poor Mencken, he has his troubles too," Fitzgerald said, pointing to a letter on the table. "He was a confirmed bachelor like Nathan, but a few years ago he married a writer, Sara Haardt was her name, who came from Montgomery, Zelda's town. She died early this summer. She suffered most of her adult life from respiratory ailments. Worse than I have with my t.b. Zelda and I were fond of her. I called Sara my favorite Venus.

"Last year Mencken knew his time had come. He quit the *Mercury* and retired to Baltimore to work on his memoirs and dictionaries. He had entertained the nation with satire through the Boom, but the Depression is no laughing matter. He made his exit at the right time. Changing conditions brought it on, but also to be with Sara that last year."

He said that Mencken declared in his retiring statement that the times needed literary men with a political and economic background. His successor was Henry Hazlitt, a literary critic who had been writing economic pieces for the *Nation* and *The New York Times*. Hazlitt had expressed his credo in *The Anatomy of Criticism:* a great writer is a traditionalist who possesses the courage to experiment, and "the social mind" was the final arbiter of literary values.

The Marxists were seeking the social mind, Fitzgerald said as he poured himself another drink. Hazlitt, more and more conservative, still agreed with their leading critic, Granville Hicks, that a writer's viewpoint was formed by social events as well as by his economic background, his limitations, and his class prejudices. But Fitzgerald made the point that great writers have always been above personal issues in the same way that they have crossed barriers of geography, nationality, time, and sex. Literature goes beyond the class struggle; it encompasses every aspect of the broadest social mind.

I could see that Fitzgerald was speaking for my benefit as a struggling writer. He had glanced at two articles I had written for Carolina papers, "Proletarian Novel in Modern Literature" and "Rebellion in the South." The first of these was sprinkled with Marxist clichés and words of praise for writers whom Fitzgerald called mediocrities. It made him so angry that he would not read through to the end. Only one of the names I mentioned seemed to please him: Robert Cantwell, the author of *The Land of Plenty.* The second article he read, or scanned, with somewhat greater interest. It was the one I had written after my interview with Olive Tilford Dargan. She had spoken at the Southern Writers' Conference at Black Mountain College, and so had Dr. Joel Spingarn, the critic and humanist, who had sounded the theme of the conference: the rebellion of Southern writers.

"To rebel is the first duty of the Southern writer at this moment when the destiny of mankind is on the industrial battlefield," Mrs. Dargan said. "The South has always been a land of rebellion. Revolt is in the blood of Southerners, as they have shown from the Mecklenburg Declaration of Independence in 1775 to and beyond the first shots of the War between the States. I believe most of us are ready now, but the question that troubles me is—how far can we go without being lynched?"

Fitzgerald was impressed by what she said about the vitality of the South and its spirit of rebellion. He was also impressed by the list of the books she had published at Scribners, the collections of poetry and plays. He wasn't so sure that he would like the proletarian novels she wrote as Fielding Burke, though the first of them, *Call Home the Heart*, had been widely praised. It is the story of a mountain girl in an industrial upheaval that resembled the famous and tragic Gastonia strike.

"I don't object to that kind of subject matter, but to the manner in which it's written, usually half-baked and unimaginative, with sensationalism instead of emotional depth and understanding," Fitzgerald said with a serious tone that alcohol sometimes made him adopt. "I realize that most bourgeois writers produce shoddy stuff and are as class-conditioned as the would-be proletarians who write about American peasants and workers. You might say they all bear the stamp of propaganda—for one class or the other—unless the books are written by poets or artists like Mrs. Dargan, Cantwell, West, or my own friends Ernest, Bunny, and Dos Passos."

That morning he was eager to make it clear that he wasn't against proletarians, but against shoddy writing of all kinds. He was born with the instincts and vitality of a rebel, he said, and he felt a closer kinship with radicals than with others. Most of his friends were politically involved; and, despite the fact that he had little time for anything but his writing and no temperament for being an activist, he had written an antiwar satire and done some speech-making in Baltimore earlier against the growing menace to world peace.

"I had communist bull sessions in our house. They annoyed Zelda, who was in and out of the hospital at that time. For two years I was on the verge of joining up, I had a visit from Jay Lovestone, who broke off from mainstream communism because of Stalin's rift with

Trotsky and started his own party. But I had no interest in or patience with ideological schisms. Instead of being drawn closer, I withdrew.

"Yes, I became disgusted with the leadership and squabbles of the two factions, and making those speeches took a lot out of me," he said, pulling out a handkerchief and wiping his forehead. "I almost went haywire those two years. I believed in the cause of peace and freedom, and the Great Change in our society that my friends were talking about, but I still felt a strong tie to my class. I wasn't able to reconcile my two loyalties, so I stepped aside and took my place on the sidelines.

"There was only enough energy for writing and personal problems," he said and went into a coughing fit. His eyes were glassy, his hands shaky, and his voice more guttural. He took a drink and wiped his face again with the handkerchief. "It's nothing—just a little cold. I have the temperament of a person who gives all or nothing. Besides, I had scoffed at politics like my good friend Mencken, and my political conscience only showed up as an element of irony in my writing. I'll tell you something. When I planned *Tender*, I intended Dick to be a communist and to send his children to study in the Soviet Union. My creative instinct took over and he emerged as a living romantic idealist. I am confident he will endure as an individual. Otherwise he would have been a type and, like most types, soon forgotten.

"A writer must find his own grain, way, bent. Like all artists he is by nature and temperament an individual and a rebel. Against society, tradition, restrictions. He aspires to create new and original works. His way is alone. If he succumbs to ideologies, he turns into a mouthpiece. He must hang on to his identity for dear life. In the end he must rely on his own judgment. It's the only way to survive as a writer and an artist."

The telephone had rung twice before he stopped. I walked over to the window as he picked it up. He listened, mumbled a few words, and hung up. When I turned to him, he seemed pleased with himself.

"It was the manager's office," he said, wiping his forehead again. "He asked his secretary to apologize and say the bellboys would bring me anything I wanted. The punk didn't have the guts to tell me himself."

I nodded and prepared to leave, saying that he ought to do something about his cold.

"I'm doing it," he said, taking another drink.

I let the matter drop and went back to his earlier subject. "What you just said sounds like something a writer friend told me when I was being rushed to join the Party. He advised me against it and warned me to watch out and hang on to my viewpoint."

"Who was that writer?"

"Mike Gold."

Fitzgerald was indeed surprised. Before I left he asked me to count his pulse while he took his temperature. I remember the count was much higher than normal and the thermometer rose above 102.

26

The following day Fitzgerald disappeared from the Inn. He didn't want anybody to know where he had gone and left instructions with the switchboard to refer all calls to his secretary. I phoned Laura a couple of times, but was unable to reach her. At last it was Lottie who phoned to tell me what had happened; she had found out from a bellhop who was on duty when Fitzgerald's doctor arrived. The doctor would take no nonsense and ordered him immediately into Memorial Mission Hospital.

Most of the time he was there I was out of town with the orchestra. I didn't see Fitzgerald until he came by the shop in October to announce that he was leaving for Baltimore. He planned to set up housekeeping for his daughter, who was going to school there, and to find an apartment where Zelda could visit them from the hospital. It was a move he looked forward to, as he hoped to make up for his "wasted summer"—he called it that with more sadness than irony.

Fitzgerald seemed to possess his old vitality and friendliness; hatless, well-groomed, and dressed in his light clothes, he was once more the college athlete or stage juvenile. There was about him the quality of a phoenix rising from its ashes. It was due to his incredible resilience, combined with a few days' rest in the hospital, where he had the benefit of sleep, solid food, no alcohol, and the attention of smiling young nurses.

"You look fine," I said in the spirit of our old intimacy.

"My doctor didn't think so. He was for keeping me there another few days. I told him I couldn't spare the time, and walked out," he said, as though pleased with himself for having disobeyed orders. "I had a close call. It was pleurisy that went into walking pneumonia because of my spotted lungs."

He went on to speak of his wasted summer, which he hoped to turn into a productive fall and winter. Lying in that hospital bed, he had reviewed his periods of activity and waste, his bouts with horror, and his perpetual resolve to stop drifting and squandering his resources. Every time he hit bottom he seemed to come to terms with himself and face the problem of his life with a strong determination to dominate it. He realized there was no one more destructive than a man who was his own worst enemy.

"Writing is the only thing I can do well. I was afraid I had lost my talent or run out of material. I haven't. I find I'm not as badly off as I had thought all summer," he said with a calm assurance that struck me as genuine. "Not that I have found a new source so much as an approach or way to dig deeper into my life and experiences. There is so much I can still do with them. I started writing something of the sort last year—without being conscious of it—in an article about my insomnia."

He was referring to "Sleeping and Waking," which I had read in *Esquire*. He wrote it in Baltimore after the disappointment over the failure of *Tender Is the Night*. "Waste and horror—what I might have been and done that is lost, spent, dissipated, unrecapturable. I could have acted thus, refrained from this, been bold when I was timid, cautious where I was rash. I need not have hurt her like that . . . nor broken myself trying to break what was unbreakable.

"The horror has come now like a storm—what if this night prefigures the night after death—what if all thereafter was an eternal quivering on the edge of an abyss, with everything base and vicious in oneself urging one forward and the baseness and viciousness of the world just ahead. No choice, no road, no hope—only the endless repetition of the sordid and semitragic. Or to stand forever, perhaps, on the threshold of life unable to pass or return to it. I am a ghost as the clock strikes four."

While lying in his hospital bed, he had thought of something else—something he could do that would please Zelda and help pay her expenses. For some time he had thought that a film could be made of *Save Me the Waltz*. Though it was a bad novel and he was glad that it had been forgotten, he thought it would make an excellent ballet film. Of course he would write the screen treatment and add what material he found necessary to translate the story to the visual medium.

"Do you have a biography of Pavlova?" he asked, looking over the shelves. "I need a little episode from her life."

"No," I said, going to another shelf. "We have plenty on the ballet, but *Nijinsky* is the only biography."

"Maybe it will do."

When he took the book from me Fitzgerald noticed a big brown volume on the same shelf. Its title on the spine was in five vertical red letters; he couldn't miss it. His eyes narrowed as he glanced at me, then he turned back to the Nijinsky book.

"Of course I can't use Zelda's tragic end in my treatment," he said in an off-hand professional tone. "It must have a happy ending or an equivalent—to make up for her failure as a dancer. A compensatory love story to balance her loss. I see two courses open to me: to make her a popular dancer in a musical or, because of her dedication to ballet, a dancer of supporting roles in companies here and abroad.

"If I don't write the script, some Hollywood hack will do what has been done and is expected of him—a reasonable facsimile of movies dealing with the dance and theater," he said, glancing back at the large red letters. "I have lived too close to the subject of Zelda's world of idiotic perfection to let anyone make a hash of her book. I want to do something authentic and worthy of her—with a feeling of invention on my part."

Fitzgerald added that he had talked to Dr. Robert S. Carroll of Highland Hospital about Zelda and, if he returned to Asheville the following year, he would put her in his hands. He was impressed by the doctor and thought Zelda would be happier in the Carolina mountains, in a hotel-like atmosphere, than she would be in a clinic in the heart of Baltimore. She would be treated more like a guest in a supervised retreat than a patient in a mental institution.

While he told me this Fitzgerald reached for the brown book; it was so heavy he had to use both hands to lift it off the shelf. The volume was bound in thick cloth and on its back was printed a hand-drawn map of Africa. It was Nancy Cunard's *Negro* anthology, which she had inscribed to me on the flyleaf and sent as thanks for my piece on Negro folklore. The book was published in England; the only copies to reach the States were those sent to its contributors—about fifty of them. I later learned that most of the printing was destroyed in a fire of mysterious origin; according to another story, it was lost in a World War II bombing.

"We met Nancy in Paris."

"And Lady Cunard?"

"Yes. She shared our dislike for her daughter. Negro writers and artists were flocking around Nancy as though she was their great white hope. The last time she was in New York, I heard she had a jazz musician. She didn't know he had a wife and some pickaninnies tucked away in a Harlem tenement." He paused as though expecting me to take issue with him. He was being purposely ugly. I was silent. "You probably don't mind."

"That's taste, not radicalism," I said, sensing his baiting mood. "Even you'll agree."

"At times," he said with a distant look in his eye, "you don't sound as if you ever lived in the Deep South."

"I reckon that's because the Civil War was over long before my folks got here to take sides," I replied, trying to reach him with what I thought was humor. "So we never shared that feeling of First Family Southerners."

"Mixing means nothing to you."

"My folks came from Sicily—the mixing bowl of the Mediterranean," I said lightly. His remark had been a statement, not a question, yet I had the uneasy feeling that he was heading for a showdown on the most sensitive issue that had arisen between us. Powerless before the challenge, I forced a smile and added, "That ought to make us one-hundred-per-cent hybrid."

He shot me a disdainful look, sat on the desk, and opened the book. After flipping a few pages he ran across my article, "Negro Folklore in North Carolina." He read the opening line and turned to the back of the volume. It was the illustrated section, containing photographs of African art, sculpture, ceremonial masks, and other folk objects of primitive and highly developed cultures.

Fitzgerald kept turning the glossy pages. Nothing seemed to interest him. Then he slowed down as he glanced at a section of Negro entertainers—Josephine Baker, Bill Robinson, Paul Robeson. He took his time looking over poetry by Langston Hughes, Sterling Brown, Countee Cullen, Jean Toomer, and Negro songs of protest collected in the Deep South by Lawrence Gellert.

"It sounds like the name of that chap on the Tryon paper who reminded me of Carl Sandburg," he said, as he read one of the songs.

I didn't know Gellert at the time, though I knew his brother Hugo from drawings in the radical press. He now turned the pages with interest; he stopped on noticing the name *Contempo* in the title of an article. It was illustrated by a photograph of Langston Hughes, his male secretary, Milton Abernethy, and me before the Chapel Hill post office. We had it taken on Federal property where all Americans could stand together despite the possibility of arousing local prejudice.

He studied the picture and then read the article, which was based on a long letter I had written to Nancy about Hughes's reception after he was invited by the playwright Paul Green and a student committee to read his poetry in Memorial Hall. He arrived during the furore over the *Contempo* issue on the Scottsboro Case, which had featured on the front page Hughes's article about Southern millowners and white prostitutes and his inflammatory poem "Christ in Alabama." There were also pieces by Theodore Dreiser, Lincoln Steffens, and John Dos Passos pleading for the eight black boys condemned to death in an Alabama prison.

We had tried to put Hughes and his companion in the Carolina Inn, where visiting artists and professors were lodged. The management politely said nothing was available, so we arranged for them to stay with a Negro minister. But we succeeded in having them dine with us at a popular restaurant on the main drag—because of their light coloring. The blow came when Hughes was forbidden to read in the Hall; there was a campus demonstration for freedom of speech and he was permitted to read elsewhere. Then local patriots got after us for having brought Negroes to dine in a lily-white café.

"Did your communist friends put you up to this?"

"It was our own idea—like asking members of the Scottsboro Defense Committee for articles."

"Dos was in on it?"

"Along with Dreiser, Steffens, Professor Boas, and Burton Rascoe," I answered, letting myself go. "Dreiser also had his own committee for the relief of the Harlan, Kentucky, striking miners. And we wrote to everybody but Rascoe."

"Rascoe—an inimical bastard." He eyes seemed to smolder, not at me this time. "A stinking parlor pink who will jump off the radical bandwagon when the wind changes. The sort of fellow traveler who kisses the asses of his social peers and beats his chest with such gibberish as Negro rights and equality."

"It's not gibberish," I said firmly, before realizing I had uttered the words so forcefully.

"Probably not to you," he said, directing his smoldering look at me. "It's the thing they were yapping about most that made me pull out of the League against This and That. And it's time you came to your senses before going the way of all our Tom Boyds. You seem to have some of his vitality and stubbornness, if not his talent, so I doubt if this will seep through that skull of yours."

"Thanks," I remember saying, more angry than hurt. "I know you hate Rascoe's guts. Perhaps for good reason. Didn't he pan *Gatsby* and praise the barnyard boys?"

The question caught him off guard. His face flushed. Then something that must have rankled him for weeks came to mind, and he flung it at me.

"You said you put me in the Big League! But you never mentioned me! In your tribute to Faulkner, you praised him as our top writer—above Dreiser, Anderson, Ernest, and Dos. You left me out, like all the others!"

"Maybe because you didn't answer us."

"You said Ernest didn't either."

"True," I said lamely, and then I remembered. "In that tribute we left out Wolfe too—and he's a Chapel Hill legend."

"You're slippery as an eel," he said a bit more calmly. "You'll make a top press agent and you know what I think of them."

"Yes, a glorified pimp on the expense account."

Fitzgerald nodded with a pleased look on his face. That was his line, all right. He stalked out of the shop, forgetting to take the Nijinsky book with him. (It wasn't the copy in which I wrote notes of our earlier chat and, later, about this visit too.)

After he left I went back to the desk, unsettled by this whole exchange. I reached for the Cunard anthology to put it away; its weight reminded me of something that might have amused Fitzgerald. In the worst days of the Depression, I used the heavy volume as an overnight presser—to put a crease back into my only pair of pants.

27

I see in retrospect that, by the end of the year, Fitzgerald had summoned up enough self-discipline to emerge from his wasted summer into one of his mature periods as a writer. He wrote a story, "Image on the Heart," that balanced an old score with Zelda, and he wrote "The Crack-Up," a series of three confessional articles that marked the end of his old self and the dawn of the new. His vitality and amazing resilience had pulled him up from the depths.

The story, which has not been reprinted—though it deserves to be—was published in *McCall's*, April 1936. It closed an episode in his emotional life that had tormented him for a decade: Zelda's brief affair with a French aviator, the one she described in *Save Me the Waltz*. Fitzgerald had committed himself to her with a romantic love akin to adoration. In the light of that love her infidelity had seemed to him incredible and even ridiculous; it had shattered his sense of trust and identity.

His writer's instinct functioned with a sense of moral balance both in his work and in his personal life. Thus, in *Tender Is the Night*, Fitzgerald gives Nicole the right to have an affair with Tommy Barban to balance her husband's affair with Rosemary. In his own life Fitzgerald required such a liaison in order to compensate for Zelda's adultery. He had to balance their position in order to strengthen his shaken ego and pride as a man.

Zelda's hold on his romantic imagination made it hard for him to find a satisfactory partner for such a compensatory act. Desperately he tried to find such a partner before and after her breakdown. Love was a rare emotion for him, and the sexual act without at least an illusion of love seemed to him a mere compulsion, an ugly thing. His own "Rosemary" was the first woman to reawaken love in him, for a time, and the only one to make him forget Zelda. Rosemary, despite her shortcomings, had given him a renewed feeling of youth, energy, confidence, and hope in the future. Whether or not the love she aroused in him was an illusion, the affair served its purpose. No relationship other than that with Zelda had plunged him into such despair after it ended. Rosemary played an important role in liberating him from emotions of the past so that he might function as his new self.

Briefly summarized, "Image on the Heart" is the story of an American girl in France who, like Zelda, falls in love with a French aviator. The romance takes place a week before she is to marry an American there. She gives up her aviator and marries the American as planned, but her husband will always wonder about her and the marriage can never be what it might have been. The parallel is unmistakable, for Zelda, too, gave up her aviator and went on living with Fitzgerald, but their relationship was never again to be the same. The story has the same nostalgic overtone as the closing paragraph of "Winter Dreams," in which the hero says to himself those words that Fitzgerald had repeated to me: "Long ago, there was something in me, but now that thing is gone. Now that thing is gone, that thing is gone. I cannot cry. I cannot care. That thing will come back no more."

The "Crack-Up" articles go beyond the scope of his earlier "Sleeping and Waking" and mark the birth of a new writer in Fitzgerald. He is once again his own protagonist, but writes of himself with wry humor and more detachment than before. There is indeed a residue of bitterness, self-reproach, and bravado masquerading as studied indifference, so that he is not always able to maintain objectivity, but he is well on his way to achieving it.

The first of the articles (*Esquire*, February 1936) describes the self-confidence of the old Fitzgerald, to whom "Life was something you dominated if you were any good. Life yielded easily to intelligence and effort," and he was sure he had plenty of both. But he was living too hard, and one day, at the age of thirty-nine, he "sat in the office of a great doctor and listened to a grave sentence." It didn't overwhelm him; he simply went to a little town, slept or dozed twenty hours a day, and tried not to think. Then suddenly, surprisingly, he got better—"And cracked like an old plate as soon as I heard the news." The savor went out of his life and he felt a loss of vitality. "Of all natural forces," he says, "vitality is the incommunicable one."

The second article (March 1936) is the further history of a cracked plate. "Sometimes [it] has to be retained in the pantry, has to be kept in service as a household necessity. It can never again be warmed on the stove nor shuffled with the other plates in the dishpan; it will not be brought out for company, but it will do to hold crackers late at night or to go into the ice box under left-overs." Fitzgerald tells us that he went into a period of silence during which he was impelled to think. "God, was it difficult!" he says. "The moving about of great secret trunks." He decided that he had allowed other men to act as his conscience and that "there was not an 'I' any more—not a basis on which I could organize my self-respect—save my limitless capacity for toil that it seemed I possessed no more."

Such hope as remained is set forth in the third article (April 1936). Those who survive, he says, make a "clean break . . . something you cannot come back from . . . because it makes the past cease to exist." For Fitzgerald this meant that he had shucked off "the old dream of being an entire man in the Goethe-Byron-Shaw tradition, with an opulent American touch, a sort of combination of J. P. Morgan, Topham Beauclerk and St. Francis of Assisi." "I have now become a writer only," he says. What he does not say in the article, but what it implies in terms of his life, is that his new writing is to come from the matured memory of a deep experience; from digging within himself.

By the time the "Crack-Up" articles appeared, I had sold the Asheville bookshop and moved to New York. Hallie Flanagan, who knew my *Contempo* work, had asked me to edit a *Federal Theatre Magazine*, then being planned as a house organ for the national project. After a year I switched to the publicity department and served an apprenticeship as a Broadway press agent. Though I was never to see Fitzgerald again, I have thought of him through the years as a friend and as the most positive influence in my efforts to become a writer worthy of receiving his advice. But I was rarely able to collect my pay as a publicist without hearing him say with scorn, "A glorified pimp on the expense account!"

Fitzgerald was back in Asheville that spring. He moved Zelda into Highland Hospital, where she spent most of her time until her death there in a fire (1948). In 1937 he was in Asheville again, before setting out for Hollywood, where his agent had gotten him a film-writing contract. He had failed in Hollywood twice before; his failures had rankled him for almost a decade. He was going back to beat the setup that had conspired against him and to earn money enough to pay his debts. Even if *Save Me the Waltz* didn't materialize as a film, he would be working for a major studio.

Before he went, and while working on his first films, Fitzgerald was to suffer two more staggering reverses—both due to his fatal flaw. But he was to conquer it, convinced as he was that he could survive only as a writer. He was no longer a man divided.

The fall day that Fitzgerald left for Baltimore, Lottie picked me up at the symphony office. With the frisky poodles at her feet, she seemed as chic—if not as gay—as her old self, but standing away from them she lost a bit of her insouciance. That morning her high-cheeked, narrow face was lined and more tanned than I could remember; a frown brought out the face of a woman, a smile that of a girl. She was more woman than girl and there was an uneasiness about her that I pretended not to notice.

Lottie had come to talk about Fitzgerald, that was obvious. She had no friends that I knew of, other than Fitzgerald and myself, and he had served as a link to bring us closer. I invited her for coffee, but she preferred to sit in the sun outside the Arcade. Morning was her bed-time; I could tell she hadn't slept. Whatever was troubling her, I knew it involved him. This was the last time I saw her; I don't know where she went, but it couldn't have been Baltimore.

"He talked about reforming—not me, but himself," she said with the pretense of a laugh. "He's too old for such tricks as three-day bats. He can't take it any more. He said he had aimed to drink himself to death, but thought it cowardly, and decided not to—out of pride. Now a new life is waiting for him in Baltimore with his family. No more drinking and women, the two things that get him into trouble. It'll be a big change for him. Work only from now on. Think he can make it?"

"If he wants to," I said with a shrug. "He said he once gave up alcohol for a year. About women I don't know."

"He claims he's reached the point where he can take 'em or leave 'em." She paused a moment to watch her dogs lolling in the grass. "While in the hospital he thought about a lot of things. He said that a love affair seemed to free him from his wife. And he thought he could enjoy sex now—thanks to me—without thinking it was a forbidden pleasure."

"You've done him a good service."

"But he's still clumsy and shy about it even if he's learning to take his time. How screwed up can a writer be and make sense in his books?"

"The more screwed up some of them are, the more profound and brilliant they sound."

Fitzgerald told her that he was retiring to a quiet existence of work and of being a father. There would be regular meals, a writing schedule, time for play with his daughter, and long walks. The exercise would help him to sleep again without drugs; he felt these were weakening his heart, but he had to have them. The simple life excluded excitement on the outside, so he could sink deeper into his inner world.

"I'll write about you, but not as you are," Fitzgerald said to her. "I'll use bits of you, combine them with fragments of others, and come up with a character you won't recognize. I may use your temperament, your casual mood, or the feeling you leave with me. That lingers long after impressions have faded with your story."

Speaking of Zelda to Lottie, Fitzgerald once more said that he was partly responsible for her breakdown. He spoke of her, though, not with his old sense of guilt, but with an understanding that went beyond merely seeing her in a new light. Zelda was painting again, he said—odd, distorted shapes in vivid colors, all a residue of the chaos that had driven her to the ballet. Yes, he should have been more considerate of her, not chided her, not said bitter things which estranged them and forced her to take refuge in the sole company of her teacher. He was drinking heavily at the time—a time when he should have used his head instead of losing it.

"Now she reads the Bible, hanging on to every word as though seeking spiritual guidance. When I look at her, it's like seeing an apparition—the ghost of someone I once loved," he said to Lottie with detachment. "We belong to different worlds, and though we share memories of golden days we speak a different language. When I heard she was doomed, I saw myself doomed with her. But I must go on writing—the one thing I can do better than most of my contemporaries."

Lottie said he rambled on as though he expected not to see her again. Though he didn't moralize about her profession, he repeated that it gave him an uncomfortable feeling to think about it. He mentioned a novel and a short story in which the heroines were saved by holy men—only for the holy men to be destroyed by lusts of the flesh that the women had awakened in them. The novel was Anatole France's *Thaïs*, about a courtesan and a high priest in old Alexandria; the story was Somerset Maugham's "Miss Sadie Thompson," made into the play and film, *Rain*, in which an American missionary confronts a prostitute in the lush South Seas.

"I don't think I care to read them," she said with a genuine lack of interest. "They sound silly and those writers couldn't have known a thing about such girls. It's like this Lawrence. Reading his *Lady Chat*, he sounds like a schoolboy waking up to sex as not being sinful."

"You told him this?"

"Yes, but he wanted me to read *Sons and Lovers* or *The Rainbow*. Now I'm getting a kick out of John Reed. None of this nonsense in his book about love, sin, and men destroying themselves saving lost women. I hardly read before and I might stop—if that's all it's about."

Lottie rose and went to her poodles. They danced around her and she petted them a moment. When she came back with them she gazed at the far-off mountains. I got up and looked at them too. Then she spoke in a low, harsh voice. Her face was deep in a frown and I saw more lines than before. Her fingers clutched at a beaded necklace.

"He said something last night I didn't like. It was about him and you." She paused. "Well, I let him have it. I couldn't help myself. I'll never see him again. Maybe you won't either. No regrets for me. I hope you'll have none."

She gave me a sharp look. I was silent.

"It's not about your being a radical. He said he was one himself. But things radicals preach that he doesn't like." She went on slowly. "He said you were bound to meet, but didn't have to be friends. And that he had never forgotten or forgiven an injury. When I got the drift of what he meant, that finished us right then and there."

She was again silent. "He brought up the race thing and all that goes with it. Sounded sore as hell about it and you—you being stubborn while he was trying to talk sense to you. He said some of his Red friends had sold you a bill of goods. The stuff they're selling Negroes to join them and fight for their rights. A gimmick to make converts. A con game to boost membership and have them join in those marches. And another cause to scream about when asking freedom for the downtrodden masses."

Lottie spoke with emotion, but she remained calm, and with a note of sarcasm in her voice as though mimicking Fitzgerald.

"He talked like a dyed-in-the-wool Southerner, thinking I was on his side. He was mistaken. Not that I'm a Red or whatever—I never bothered to vote for any Tom, Dick, or Harry running for the White House. He didn't either, he said. But about Negroes and the ways of white folks, I happen to know plenty."

She deliberately gave the last sentence the rhythm and inflection of Southern speech—she must have been a good actress. But the revelation in her choice of words and expressions, a characteristic phrasing, escaped me then.

"When he got to yelping about radicals wanting to mix up the races, I reminded him that whites had been doing that for hundreds of years. He explained things were different and we knew better now. When I asked him what he meant, he said our race was superior and we shouldn't weaken it by mixing. The hemming and hawing was over. He was no more the famous writer to me, a man I'd slept with and liked, but a pasty-faced white kid named Jasper who used to yell, 'Mama!' every time he laid eyes on me."

Lottie paused and sat on the bench, and then went on with an odd smile. "You'd think he might've caught on to what I was—the way I'm sure you have by now. But I had to spell it out for him. I asked if he'd ever gone to bed with a colored girl. He gave me the damnedest look, like I accused him of sleeping with his sister. Before he could answer, I told him that he had. Yes, not once or twice, but a dozen times. He lost his tongue at that. So I told him if it gave him any consolation, I was three-quarters his color. When he got over that shock, he walked away like I had leprosy and told me to put on my clothes."

She continued, "He was stewing and dying for a drink. He looked for a bottle, tore up the place, slamming doors and drawers, and smashed the last empty on the floor. Then he picked up the phone and called room service for a drink. He caught my eye and canceled it. While I slipped on my skirt and blouse, he lit a cigarette with shaky hands. He took a couple of drags, and then let his face drop in his hands like he was about to bawl. He mumbled something like this over and over: 'Oh, God, what's happened to me? What's happened to me?'

"I laughed and told him he had nothing to worry about. Whatever it was it happened for the best. In my years down South, I knew a white boy wasn't a man till he smoked, got stinko under the kitchen table, and had himself a nigger gal in the barn. Well, he finally made it in real style, and he could now call himself a man."

It was the one time, I believe, when the occasion presented itself, that Fitzgerald didn't say he was "mature at last." Instead he told her with an ironic laugh, "God, that wop bastard must be laughing up his sleeve."

"I told him you didn't know what I was—so he wouldn't take it out on you." She paused. "Now he tried to apologize, saying he liked me and was always courteous to colored people. I asked him who he had known and where. It turned out he only knew maids, bellhops, pullman porters, and people like that. But not a single one out of service. Well, I told him, he had met one now. Me. He might never put me in a book, but he'd never forget me, if he lived to be a hundred."

Lottie ended with a twisted smile. That was her triumph. But the experience had hurt, I could see. Not learning again what she already knew too well, but getting it from a man she had cared for.

"Color's a blind spot with him," I said gently. "And that goes for Jews, Italians, and other foreigners. His first books are full of nasty cracks. But he told me he had changed. Now that he's free of his wife, it might happen sooner. She was from Alabama."

She rose with a sigh. "You think so?"

"Didn't you tell him he'd never forget you, if he lived to be a hundred?"

Lottie looked at me with vacant eyes, as though surrounded by a vast emptiness. She raised a gloved hand to say good-by and walked off with her poodles prancing ahead of her. Though a bit reserved, she was once more the actress playing her casual ladylike role. As I stopped at the Arcade entrance for a last look, I saw her chatting with an elegant man who had taken off his hat to her. No doubt they were chatting about Juliet and Romeo.

Index